SEVEN VERSIONS of an
AUSTRALIAN BADLAND

Ross Gibson is a writer, teacher and filmmaker whose other books include *The Diminishing Paradise*, *South of the West*, and *The Bond Store Tales*. His films include *Camera Natura*, *Dead to the World* and *Wild*. He also produces multi-media environments for museums and public spaces, and has recently completed a three-year stint as creative director, developing the Australian Centre for the Moving Image at Melbourne's Federation Square. He is now Research Professor of New Media and Digital Culture at the University of Technology in Sydney.

SEVEN VERSIONS of an AUSTRALIAN

BADLAND

ross gibson

University of Queensland Press

First published 2002 by University of Queensland Press
Box 6042, St Lucia, Queensland 4067 Australia

www.uqp.uq.edu.au

Typeset by University of Queensland Press
Printed in Australia by McPherson's Printing Group

Distributed in the USA and Canada by
International Specialized Book Services, Inc.,
5824 N.E. Hassalo Street, Portland, Oregon 97213–3640

Sponsored by the Queensland Office
of Arts and Cultural Development.

Cataloguing in Publication Data
National Library of Australia

Gibson, Ross, 1956–   .
  Seven versions of an Australian badland.

  1. Rockhampton (Qld.) — History. I. Title.

  Bibliography.

994.35

ISBN 0 7022 3349 8

I sniff a fire burning without outlet,
consuming acrid its own smoke.

John Berryman, 'Homage to Mistress Bradstreet'

Acknowledgments

I have been given great and generous help with this book.

The staff of the John Oxley Library in Brisbane have been exemplary. The same goes for the public libraries in Mackay and Rockhampton. UQP have been a pleasure to work with. A small research grant from the Literature Board of the Australia Council came at a time that proved a turning point.

I am indebted to the following individuals for the kindness and intelligence they offered the project at various times over a decade or more: John Cruthers, Tom O'Regan, Sylvia Lawson, Jane Gleeson-White, Robyn Outram, Jeff Gibson, Debbie Lee, Debra Dawes, Jelle Van Den Berg, Julian Van Den Berg, McKenzie Wark, Peter Emmett, Jane Lydon. I would also like to thank Klaus Neumann, Nicholas Thomas and Hilary Ericksen who edited a variant of 'Version 5' in their excellent UNSW Press publication entitled *Quicksands* (1999). If I have forgotten anyone equally worthy, I beg their forgiveness for the frailty of my memory.

While dwelling on remembrance, I would like to recall the generosity and friendship of the late Colin Hood.

Ultimately and joyfully, I dedicate the book with continuous love and thanks to Kathryn Bird.

Contents

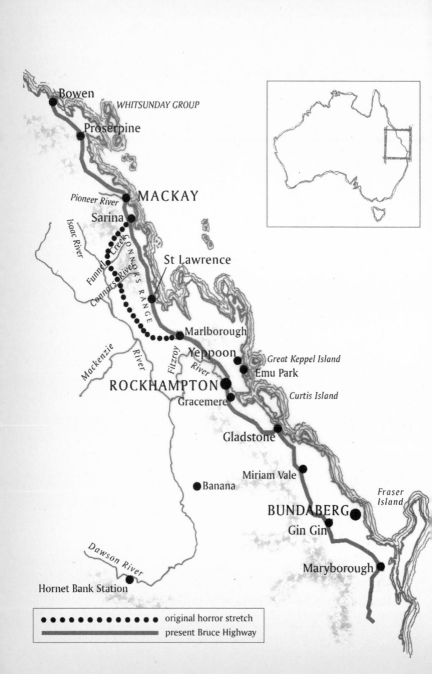

Bowen

WHITSUNDAY GROUP

Proserpine

Pioneer River

MACKAY

Sarina

Isaac River

Funnel Creek

CONNORS RANGE

Connors River

St Lawrence

Marlborough

Mackenzie River

River

Fitzroy

River

Yeppoon

Great Keppel Island

Emu Park

ROCKHAMPTON

Curtis Island

Gracemere

Gladstone

Miriam Vale

Banana

BUNDABERG

Fraser Island

Gin Gin

Dawson River

Maryborough

Hornet Bank Station

●●●●●●●●●●●●●●●● original horror stretch
━━━━━━━━━━━━ present Bruce Highway

A Beginning

Do you know the Central Queensland hinterland, the brigalow country that spooks in around when you cross the Tropic of Capricorn and travel north out of Rockhampton to the canefields of Mackay? A vast and sparse section of Australia's Pacific coast, the Capricorn country is known in popular legend as 'the Horror Stretch' — a place you're warned not to go.

Let's say you're driving there. Feeling like an alien, you skitter through thin light while the country conspires with your moods to make an emotional soundtrack for your journey. As you move through this setting, you sense fear as a bassline underscoring an air of tragedy. All the time you drive (and it takes several hours to get free of the place once it's quickened your pulses), you are haunted by fear and tragedy. For this stretch of country is an immense, historical crime-scene. In the landscape of Central Queensland, old passions and violent secrets are lying around in a million clues and traces. Whatever colonialism was and is, it has made this place unsettled and unsettling.

Between the physical geography and the 'cultural' settings that get created in imaginative tale-telling and picture-making, there always lies a landscape — a place where nature and culture contend and combine in history. As soon as you experience thoughts, emotions or actions in a tract of land, you find you're in a landscape. North of Rockhampton these contending forces have built the landscape known as the Horror Stretch. Crossing and recrossing it so curiously, you begin to understand that this 'bad' landscape might be a revelation of horrors past. You realise that badlands are not only driveable. They can be staked out in the past of a place, in a time just the other side of your immediate consciousness. Just outside the glare of your headlights.

A Daoist motto declares that 'surprise and subtle instruction might come forth from the Useless'. *Seven Versions of an Australian Badland* takes this as true for the Central Queensland badlands. After years of contemplating the Horror Stretch, I've found that this seemingly useless place never stops teaching by surprising and disturbing. It offers hard lessons about a society recovering from colonialism. It can be disturbing enough — and beautiful enough — to goad us into thinking more boldly about how the past produces the present. This remembering is something good we can do in response to the bad in our lands.

RECENTLY

Version 1

Land Gone Wrong

In March 1986, fishermen working the ocean off Rock-hampton found themselves in a Salvador Dali painting. The water was tinged milky-grey and clotted with the white bellies of thousands of dead fish. In the pungent air, a parade of goblins floated past: shetland ponies bloating to donkey size; a mad carousel of angora goats matted with red clay and threaded together by barbed fencing wire; zebu cattle gassed up and bobbing like ocean-mines, some of them exploding in the sharp morning sun. Sharks were cruising about, glutting on the feast. A fisherman remembered hearing all those thwacking jaws: a noise like a team of axemen working in a rainy forest. And overseeing everything as if spying on the sleep of reason, a motor-tricycle waded on out-sized knobbly tyres, its headlamp an unshockable eye.

A couple of weeks earlier, Tropical Cyclone Winifred had attacked the Central Queensland coast, and now the Fitzroy and Mackenzie Rivers were spewing out everything indigestible that they had guzzled when their floodwaters took the inland plains. In recent years, graziers had grown cocky, lulled into complacency by high yields of wheat and cattle. Emboldened by the good years, they had stocked right up to the river banks. But now the country had weltered on the settlers and millions of dollars of assets were afloat.

A helicopter beamed its pictures to my television in a distant city. The 'Horror Stretch' was in the news again, returning to popular attention as it does every few years, presenting itself simultaneously as an absurdity and an epiphany. The TV report brought back questions that have come to me thousands of times. How to account for this strange place, this 'Horror Stretch'? What kind of setting is it? What omen?

No single answer suffices, but this is a start: it is a tract of land that went bad. It went bad in its tropical ecology and in the minds of the many generations of people who have told tales about it.

And who are its people?

A great brawl of humanity has lived here. During the 1860s the Aboriginal clans along the Fitzroy and Pioneer Rivers saw Scottish, English and Norwegian land-grabbers ride in on the beasts called horses, to be followed a few months later by big mobs of sheep herded by nervous Irish farm workers brandishing machetes and axes. Within a few wet seasons the sheep sickened. Then beef cattle were driven on to the scrubby plains around Rockhampton while near Mackay, and to the north, sugar cane was planted in riverine tracts soon to be tended by thousands of Melanesian labourers. As the decades reeled away, Singhalese labourers and Chinese gold prospectors and market-gardeners also entered the district ahead of Italian peasants looking for the new-world chance. Soon Maltese families also began to jostle for work in the sugar country. And later, in the aftermath of World War II, Greek, Slavic and Scandinavian proletariat were to settle and struggle there too.

Nowadays vestiges of all these different lives persist in a place that has developed social turbulence matching the weather which periodically deranges the country.

squall and calm

Ecological imbalances intensified in the country after World War II when new land-claimers arrived hoping to make the place submit at last to industrial-scale agriculture. During the 1940s and 50s, farmers took to the country with prodigious aggression. They ring-barked millions of brigalow trees and left them to wither through summer. Come winter, platoons of men re-entered the paddocks and commenced burning, bull-dozing and drenching with arsenic pentoxide. Bone-coloured tree-trunks leaned about sickly, like battle casualties. Truly, it looked as if war had come to the plains. In fact many of the new farmers wielding spray-guns were ex-soldiers who had taken up land grants from the federal government when the armed forces were demobilised after the Japanese surrender. The farmers purchased cannon trailers and Matilda tanks from government war surplus sales and began blitzing the scrub, pushing blades, grading, rolling, dragging and dousing. Light planes bombed the country with a brew called 245-T and Tordon, which are alternative names for Agent Orange. These battles were to last decades.

By the 1970s, enough scrub had been scoured away to make wheat cultivation seem viable. Huge acacia tracts were denuded and farmers planted record acreages of grain. No-one was aware that the plough blades were chopping and spreading the tree roots in segments which lay in the soil like time-bombs ready to sprout millions of shoots when the right kind of rain came. For a few years, fantastic wealth was reaped from the fresh nitrogenous fields which had been made fertile by the legume-nodules of the brigalow. Stock were auctioned off and fences were pulled down to increase the extent of wheat runs. The country shone like a vast gold coin.

But the grain yields began to decline as each annual crop sucked draughts of nitrogen from a topsoil which now carried no brigalow to replenish the fertility. The earth tarnished from gold to dusty grey. Cyclones howled in. Floods washed entire empires into the rivers. After which the sun baked the slurry into a ceramic shield. Farmers then felt as scalded and exposed as the country. They realised that they could not return to running cattle because they had destroyed their own fences and dams during the wheat boom. Then after the ruin they saw the acacia profusely sprouting again from the ploughed-in root fragments, and they saw the surviving cattle bellying down in mud whenever the rains came back. Faced with the enormity of all that can go bad, many battlers simply went AWOL, leaving the tanks and mortgaged tractors to rust, where some can still be found today, completely demobilised at last. With each new rainy season, machines settle a little more obstinately on their axles.

Meanwhile, in the sugar country at the northern end of the brigalow, the canegrowers have fared only a little better. Decade by decade they have tried to dodge between drought and drenching. Each summer, big rain squalls assail the coastline. Wind tears at buildings and pasture. Water swells the hundreds of creeks that vein the hinterland between the Pacific coast and the Dividing Range. If the squalls intensify into cyclones, lashings of ocean get shoved further west across the mountains, slathering the coastal plain on the way out to the inland erosion-country where the rain abates eventually, just as the floods begin to surge.

Cyclones are the turbines that generate Central Queensland floods. They come three or four times per decade. January 1918 is the standard that every season gets measured against. In Mackay, ugly weather heaved up the Pioneer River, sucking ocean in behind it and expelling a tidal wave over the massive sand catchment at the river mouth. Gales funnelled the sea into the Pioneer Valley. It was like a huge set of bellows attached to a leaky hose. In the explosion of water, thirty people were drowned. Train and tram tracks, bridges, road-work, canefields, mills and houses were all thrashed south and west onto the brigalow country.

At the time of this deluge, a stoic, poetic man called George Randall was the lighthouse keeper on Flat Top Island, which is a rocky crumb choking the mouth of the Pioneer River. In the first blast of the cyclone, his shuddering stone cottage had been unroofed and he had huddled under debris while the cyclone refused to pass. When the winds abated two days later and 'the weather settled down thick & rainey', Randall toured the island with a notebook. He found that 'the entire shoreline was altered' and 'the beach was strewn with thousands of dead birds & also fish of all de-scriptions, including several large sharks and rock cod; many birds, though still alive, were too exhausted to move'. The earth had undergone a sea-change. In the following days most of the stockpiled sugar from the prodigious storage sheds of Mackay dissolved in the flooded, broken buildings. Fragrant syrup oozed into the streets and as the sun re-emerged the town baked slowly into a sticky pudding besieged by billions of gorging bees. A huge humming muzzled the coast for a fortnight.

Enormous climatic surges have blustered each generation of newcomers who have tried to belong in Central Queensland. Squall and calm chase each other down the decades. Such weather is endemic to the Stretch and it underwrites human experience so that violence begins to seem natural. In its ecosystems, in its social systems, this place always seems ready to convulse.

made by imaginations

North of Rockhampton, you find this landscape where people are warned not to go. The tales told of this place suggest it is a lair for evil, either because malevolence flourishes naturally there, or because trouble has been shoved in there since colonial times, mustered and corralled there by the orderly settlements that have gradually been established in the gentler regions all around the brigalow. It's a badland clumping near the good and lawful land of greater Australia.

'Badlands' is a term coined two centuries ago in North America in response to a dreadful sense of insufficiency felt by Europeans forging into the more 'savage' parts of the 'new' world. The word originally applied to an extensive, parched tract of Dakota, where erosion had sculpted the plains into a griddle of ravines and ridges that were described by early French travellers as *mauvaises terres à traverser* (bad lands to cross). Therefore a badland was originally a tract of country that would not succumb to colonial ambition.

In modern times, the connotations of the word have been bloodied by a trail of murders that were strewn across the states of Nebraska and Wyoming when a disturbed young man named Charley Starkweather stormed into the news during 1958. In one of the first live-television narrations of a criminal manhunt, an international audience followed the depredations of Starkweather and his fourteen-year-old girlfriend, Carole Fugate. They were dubbed the 'badlands killers'. (Two decades later they would become the subjects of Terrence Malick's majestic film, *Badlands*.) While bodies were discovered in farmhouses, wells and cars across the Great Plains, a communal panic was reported and redoubled in radio testimonies and gossip so that by the time Starkweather was apprehended, interviewed and syndicated, the mobile rampager had become an archetype in the mass-media bestiary.

Tales of murder and itinerancy in wild country are as old as the story of Cain in the killing-fields of Eden. But why do we still attend to stories of badlands? What cordons off these troublesome territories and highlights them so dramatically? A wrathful god? The devil? Nature following its own laws? Or fate, perhaps? No, badlands are made by imaginations that are prompted

14

by narratives. A badland is a narrative thing set in a natural location. A place you can actually visit, it is also laid out eerily by your mind before you get there. It is a disturbing place that you feel compelled to revisit despite all your wishes for comfort or complacency.

Most cultures contain prohibited or illicit spaces, but no-go zones are especially compelling within *colonial* societies. By calling a place ominous and bad, citizens can admit that a pre-colonial kind of 'savagery' lingers inside the colony even though most of the country has been tamed for husbandry and profit.

To own up to a badland may seem defeatist, like an admission that the habitat cannot be completely conquered. But a prohibited space can also appear encouraging to the extent that it shows that savagery can be encysted even if it cannot be eliminated. A badland can be understood as a natural space deployed in a cultural form to persuade citizens that unruliness can be simultaneously acknowledged and ignored. This is the kind of paradox that myths usually support. In a culture unconvinced of its sovereignty in the landscape, a badland is mythic and far from useless.

human limits

Australia's most famous badland has long been the 'dead centre' of the outback. Charles Sturt's descriptions of the terrain he explored west of the Murrumbidgee during the 1830s are definitive. His journals depict a landscape without solace:

> It is impossible for me to describe the kind of country we were now traversing, or the dreariness of the view it presented. The plains were still open to the horizon, but here and there a stunted gum tree, or a gloomy cypress, seemed placed by nature as mourners over the surrounding desolation. Neither beast nor bird inhabited these lonely and inhospitable regions, over which the silence of the grave seemed to reign.

In the paragraphs that follow this description, Sturt becomes the consummate myth-maker, manipulating his reader's anxieties, paradoxically sounding ominous at the same time as he is consoling. At the edge of this void, he explains how he encountered his own human limits (which stood for the colony's social limits) and then he transcended them — after the anxiety comes the solace. For even though these wastelands are undeniable and intractable, they must be understood to be negligible in comparison to the benign territories which had been successfully settled all over the colony. By highlighting these desolate, impenetrable regions momentarily, Sturt could encourage colonists with his memories of the more lively portion of the continent. Readers could thus acknowledge a sense of vulnerability and incapacity whilst sequestering their qualms in a restricted zone which they could ignore so long as they stayed within the well-husbanded majority of the settlement.

The myths of the Horror Stretch work in a similar way. The isolation of this landscape, its eeriness, its narratives of violence all set the Capricorn scrub apart from the rest of the Queensland coast. It is a place where evil can be banished so that goodness can be credited, by contrast, in the regions all around. It's our own local badland, a place set aside for a type of story that we still seem to need.

Version 2

Ghosts

'Have you known IMMODERATION? … PROFLI-
GACY? … Did you ever add LASSITUDE on top of
IMMODERATION? My friends, are you ready for
the questions God will put to you?'

I'm convinced I heard a man say this. Privately, I've
always called him 'the preacher'. There's a chance it
was just a dream: me as a ten-year-old, bleary in the
back seat of a car heading north out of Rockhampton.
The radio too loud for comfort in the stupefying heat
of Central Queensland. Admittedly, during most of
our trips along this desolate stretch of road, I was in
that low-level delirium of carsickness, boredom and
dread that suffused many Australian children's vacations
during the 1960s.

But for the important things, I like to think I was
awake.

in pursuit of the car

For example, I remember my eyes widening when I saw 'the ghosts'. It was late afternoon, and the altering sunlight was basting the cattle runs southwest of the Sarina Range as we skittered toward Mackay. I was playing 'nodding-dog', kneeling face-backwards, chin resting on the shelf of the car's rear window. Which meant I could watch the road peel away into the evening gloom. During this particular sunset, we were fizzing through a fragrant strip of country recently doused by a storm that the ocean had flicked on to the hot brigalow plain. As we began to climb the mountain range, the sun was a moodlight following us, and the tarmac was hot with the waning day. Each time the road bent at a special angle, the slanted sun showed me columns of steam twisting up, man-sized, in pursuit of the car. Five or six of them stalking us for a few heartbeats. Then the car would take a bend and the ghosts would vanish momentarily. But at the next curve they came back, like a reward for my attentiveness. What made them more special was that my parents were looking the wrong way. They were in the front seat, peering into the immediate future, and would not have been persuaded to kink around even if I'd thought to insist. To my child-mind, I'd been offered a special haunting — as alluring as it was frightening — about where we had come from. By the time we made it to Mackay, the night was installed and I no longer had the back-light for seeing the ghosts. But ever after I've maintained a sense of them always being present in the tropical air.

By this stage of my child-life I'd heard scores of Horror Stretch legends, and I could never decide if the scrub actually was evil or if it was just the stories shivering my young mind. But I also remember how everything was real — the ghosts truly were there at the same time as they were just steam.

preacher's breath

The ghosts appeared during the same trip I heard the preacher. I recall him in vivid detail, as the radio blarped out his voice, a little like a trumpet solo from the ABC Radio jazz programs that sometimes accompanied us through the brigalow. But this time we had a weak-signalled local station, our extended antenna hooking it by chance. Static seared the preacher's voice occasionally as the transmission bounced and scrambled off the distant ridges. His timbre was broad like a cattleman's, but pointed too, like a believer's. I also recall seeing a church. A rudimentary shed with COME TO THE LORD painted on both sides of a steeply pitched roof. I can't be certain if this was during the ghost-trip, or later. But twenty years afterwards, I drove up there to check, and the church was still standing in the hard light, rust eating like temptation at the old corrugated iron.

Even now, I can recall the sound of the preacher's breathing, as it cut through the noise of the engine and the simmering bitumen road. Each breath rasped as he sucked it in before barking a new phrase:

WHAT WAS YOUR POISON? Friends, God will ask you this question. What was your poison? What remains in a dead sinner's body? He will look to your residue, to your body and soul. What vile evidence have you left behind you? What will stay and tell in your dead sinner's body? What wastage? What chemistry? What marks of addiction? What damage? What malignancy? What signs of corruption?

Friends, we do not have a normal man's task here. So we cannot have a normal man's energies. Friends, we have a special God here, and the Devil is mighty almost to match him. God gives us our energies. But the Devil gives us our appetites. We must govern them strongly, or Satan will devour us.

Friends, you can see it in our region. I mean the OVER-RIPENESS. The PROFLIGATE sensual anarchy. Are you an idle pleasure-seeker? Do you know the sickly fruits of indulgence? Do you pry and enquire past all good limits? Do you disregard boundaries? Such is our history, this OVER-REACHING. Such is our shame in the annals of the Lord!

Friends, if we don't learn about abstinence, we go back to the wilderness. Ask yourself now, are you lulled in your senses? Do you know this rythym? 'SQUALL AND TORPOR! SQUALL AND TORPOR!' Can you feel it now, can you feel it cradle and slow you? Will you loll in LASSITUDE all through the Lord's September? He'll send January cyclones so you'll hear him and fear him!

We must look to His authority. We must husband our urges. We must own up to our history of lapsing in the annals of the Lord.

WHAT IS YOUR POISON? For some souls in our region it is gold that has damned them. GOLD! A root for all evil. Veins of poisonous concentrate cancerous in our mother the earth.

Other sinners have craved SPACE and nothing more. Avaricious land-grabbers and water-leachers, these space-hunters came in uninvited.

OPIUM also has laid too many low. Pagan gypsy Chinese and hapless blacks in mutual damnation.

But what of you and ALCOHOL? This poison you tolerate, is it any less wicked?

Friends, you must purge yourself now of the Devil's addictions. You must come to the Lord in your regional church. Come to the people who know you and who'll save you. Discount now the blots that sully your past. Come to the Lord in your regional church.

I don't want gifts tonight. I want SACRIFICE!

He went on like that, as I wound down the window to sniff the next incoming storm. It must have been 1966. I would have been ten years old. You could say I was just impressionable. But if you drive the Stretch nowadays, the preacher's travelogue still fits the land-

23

scape well — ghostly impressions and intimations of repercussion smudging the peripheries of your consciousness in the late afternoon heat.

Version 3

Fatality

March 22, 1975. This was the year Noel Weckert got serious about skydiving. It made him want to *shout*. Him and Life and Death negotiating in the fierce North Queensland sky. He'd even started wondering if he could make a living from it. Getting paid to hit the ground running, nerves all ablaze. Who'd choose to be a salesman?

What's more, it was something he could do with the wife. Something they were equally good at.

So he and Sophie were driving down from Townsville for the jumpers' carnival at Rockhampton. They were going to be judges, but they'd get to dive too. Stepping out into the clouds, you figure the odds. Attentiveness over Gravity. There was a joke for the first-timers: nothing in the air can hurt you … it's what happens on the ground you've got to worry about.

white-lining

It was Friday, night-time. Noel had grizzled about a speeding ticket they'd snagged outside Home Hill. Then they'd listened to the radio jabber through the crackle as lightning whacked the mountain ranges. Malcolm Fraser had just moved on Bill Snedden and become federal leader of the Opposition. Picked him off clinically, the radio said.

South of Mackay, the signal would have gone out of range, so there'd have been not much distraction other than the familiar clicks and creaks of the old Toyota Celica. Noel at the wheel. Getting twitchy in the legs. Sophie watching the country outside. And growing sleep-hungry too. Scanning the country left and right. Snarls of barbed wire; light bouncing off roofing iron; an old wheel-less tractor stooped down like a horse in need of killing. Or she could just close her eyes and breathe minutes of nothing. Nothing you'd give a name to. Looking out again she'd have seen cattle staring stupidly at the road. There must be people who live here. But who'd choose to?

Leaving the canefields behind, they'd coasted through Sarina and then chugged up the densely wooded range till they accelerated over the crest and dropped westerly into dusty air. Gone now the iodine tang in the sea-breeze that had followed them up the gradient.

With the coastal plain behind them, they etched a

line through the flatland rain-shadow while a stingy wind drifted in from the outback mining country. There'd be three or four hours of this to Marlborough and then they'd get a half-hour of double-lane highway into Rockhampton. But till then the road would punctuate their tedium with sudden staccatos of corrugation. Twenty times a narrow bridge would yelp against the tyres before Noel realised the car had been funnelled briefly into a single-lane creek-crossing. Other times, the car would dip through the sudden subsidences where washaway gullies had chewed at the bitumen each time the rains had come through during the past year or so. And always enveloping them, the flatlands on each side of the road, scrubbing the eyes with the samey grey-greenness of clumping acacia trees.

By the time they reached Connors River, halfway across the stretch between Mackay and Rockhampton, they'd been white-lining it for nine hours, and sleep was grabbing at them both. So they peed in the bushes, eased the seats back and settled in for a reviving nap till sunrise would doubtless wake them with its headachey glare.

.22 calibre

The Celica was noticed beside the camber a few hours later, in the fomenting sunlight. Only Noel's body was in it. Seatbelted still. He'd bled from the .22 calibre rifle-shots in his neck and head. A truck driver had reported the mess at dawn and roadblocks were up within an hour.

This was big news. It made the front pages in the metropolitan newspapers. TV crews. Phone-links for radio. Helicopters. It was the Horror Stretch again. Editors permitted reporters some poetic details: the Weckerts' silky terrier was said to have been found cowering under the Celica, having recently watched the killers take Sophie away; bullet marks studded nearby roadsigns; crows were moaning commentaries all round the roadblock, their noise — like the terrier's barking and the previous night's gunshots — getting sucked quickly into the massed silence of the brigalow trees. The papers made much of the names accorded to landmarks nearby: the Styx River, Charon Point, Grave Gully, the Berserkers Range, a cattle run called Tartrus.

Eight stockmen on horseback turned up to trawl the Connors River. Seventy police and volunteers assembled in all kinds of vehicles. The Mackay District Motor Cycle Club arrived, followed by the Eimeo Bushrangers Club.

This last detail was poignant. Three years earlier, a fourteen-year-old Eimeo girl had disappeared on her way to school. Her brothers, dawdling just minutes behind, had found her bike and school-bag in a shallow gully on the edge of a canefield. At the time, some

TV reports had described how the bike's front wheel was still spinning when the boys discovered it. The Eimeo case had spotlighted the township harshly and the crime remained a traumatic mystery. So the locals were using this new incident to work on the pain.

The Mackay *Mercury* mentioned that Connors River was close by Funnel Creek where a double murder had occurred not long ago. Now reporters were speculating about a pattern, possibly a serial killer. The region was staging another of its bleak melodramas. Local papers and the Brisbane *Courier-Mail* all did the tally: at least six murder investigations in six years along this most isolated section of the national highway, and there may have been more killings that were unknown as yet.

In an editorial headlined 'A HORROR STRIP!' the *Mercury* wondered what was in the atmosphere that caused 'every new road sign erected to assist motorists on the highway [to be] peppered with small arms fire almost from the moment it is put up and no one ever sees this happening'. The editor went on to describe how locals were now arming themselves when travelling the road. A letter from a local shire councillor offered an equation: 'There appeared to be a direct relationship between numbers murdered and an increase in traffic volume and unhappily we appear to be importing a problem which I expect to worsen if direct and drastic action is not taken.' The Rockhampton *Morning Bulletin* maintained the xenophobic tone, declaring that this road, where a policeman had recently been stalked by a sniper with a high-powered rifle, was a 'haunt' for 'dropouts' who drifted through from the larger cities to the south and the north.

Politicians started reciting monologues. The *Morning Bulletin* reported a Rockhampton councillor's demand for regular police patrols to 'flush out the criminal element which were marauding the road'. He recalled how, eight years previously, another Rockhampton councillor had dubbed the highway 'a bitumen tight-rope' and had condemned the state government for wilfully endangering Central Queenslanders.

By the time Noel Weckert died, therefore, the country itself was cast as a serial killer. The Brisbane papers elaborated the theme. Four days after the Celica had been found, the *Telegraph* ran an article entitled 'You Can't Trust Anyone'. It recounted the misfortunes of Joyce and Ron Linfoot in September, 1967. Hauling a caravan, the English holiday-makers had pulled up beside Princhester Creek, not far from Connors River. Ron climbed out to stretch his legs and was cut down by a bullet hitting his spine. As he lay in the dirt, he scrabbled a rifle from under the seat of the car. Meanwhile, Joyce was knocked sideways by a bullet thudding her shoulder. Within seconds, Ron got the gun firing. Startled to have branches and rocks exploding around them, the assailants fled into the bush as Ron reloaded and dragged himself into the van. During the eerie lull that followed, Joyce hauled herself into the driver's seat and tore the quiet apart by revving out of the ambush as Ron slid across the floor of the fishtailing van, sniping out the door as they lit out for Rock-hampton.

The *Telegraph* explained how this crime-scene was just a gunshot away from the site where, a year before the Linfoots, a man described in court as 'an aggressive psychopath' had killed a camper and wounded two companions. This earlier case is classic Horror Stretch. It became known as the 'Lotus Creek Outrage'.

---

pausing to load the rifle behind a tree

Three young men — two brothers named Robertson, from Sydney, and a Victorian youth called Metcalf — had been working their way north along the Queensland coast, finishing up in Townsville in the brewing heat of late October. Resolving to make it home for Christmas, they filled up the brothers' old car and started the big southern haul. The first night, exhaustion flagged them down along the Stretch, and they pulled up to doss in a paddock.

Meanwhile, an eighteen-year-old youth was night-riding back and forth from his base-camp at Connors River, where he'd been living since drifting up from Sydney three or four months earlier. (Because he is back in ordinary life nowadays, we'll give him a fictitious name: Bremner.) During the last few weeks, Bremner had been working as a fettler in the railyard at St Lawrence. That Friday night, he'd already driven from work to camp, and on to Mackay, then to Sarina, back to Connors River, then south to Lotus Creek before heading for Rockhampton. FRIDAY NIGHT! To start the weekend, he was looking to get some value out of the Stretch. So he got drinks and petrol at one roadhouse and stopped at another to pick up some ammo for the .22 rifle he'd bought from a workmate earlier in the week.

Not far out of Lotus Creek, fatal moonlight glinted off the windscreen of the Sydney boys' parked car as Bremner belted past. He cruised a hundred yards, braked, thought, and walked back — pausing to load the rifle behind a tree.

One of the Robertsons was in a sleeping-bag beside the car. Bremner woke him and shot him. A cry of fright burst from inside the car and the startled Bremner spun and popped a shot through the window. This killed the other Robertson boy immediately, and flying glass lacerated Metcalf in the seat behind. Bremner reloaded and pumped another shot into the sleeping-bag at his feet. The next reload jammed the breech at the same time as Metcalf churned out of the car, yelling and bleeding.

Bremner ran off. To Metcalf's stinging eyes it looked as if the killer just stepped into the darkness, the way you might jump out of a plane — so sudden and complete was his going, to match the way he'd appeared out of nowhere.

Out in that darkness, when Bremner climbed into his concealed car, he waited a few moments, and then made a slow U-turn. His spotlights lit up the scene: Metcalf was chugging the brothers' jalopy out of the sandy verge. He had a dead man beside him, a dying one wrapped in a sleeping-bag on the seat behind. Just as he was noticing how tacky with blood the steering wheel felt, his old car coughed to a stop in the middle of the road.

Then Bremner cruised up, smiling. Metcalf beamed back at him thankfully, thinking this was a newcomer, thinking the nightmare was over and this fellow must have passed the gunman going in the other direction. A lucky man! Here was help from a lucky man.

Together they hauled the Robertsons over to Bremner's car. But when Metcalf paused for a calming breath, he glanced back to see Bremner shove the Robertsons out onto the bitumen and take off, spitting gravel and slewing back around toward Rockhampton. (Bremner said in court later that he had suddenly realised that his rifle was under the seat, where it would have been difficult to reach quickly when he needed it.) Metcalf ran to his stranded car, grabbed his own rifle and cranked a few shots in the direction of Bremner's disappearing vehicle. But he didn't want to use all the bullets there and then. Long minutes of bleeding followed, until the next car really was rescue. They loaded the Robertsons in, and headed for Marlborough.

Further down the road, Bremner hid his gun in a cattle paddock and took off for Rockhampton. Around midnight he tried to wake his fifteen-year-old girlfriend at her hostel, but it was locked up, so he hugged the steering wheel and snared some sleep.

In the morning, Bremner and the girl drove to Yeppoon beach where they met a few of his offsiders from the Connors River camp. After a swim and some booze, they drove back to Rockhampton and then to the Keppel Sands resort where the beach radio was broadcasting descriptions of a car wanted in relation to a murder on the inland road. With the sun going down Bremner drove the girl back to Rockhampton and then headed for Connors River, retrieving the rifle on the way. About eight kilometres from the camp, he ran out of petrol. The mates he'd run into at Yeppoon came past around 11 p.m. They all took some pot-shots at a couple of kangaroos and then Bremner picked a fight with the driver, who told him to walk it off. Left alone again, he fired a few more shots at roadsigns till he hailed a passing car and cadged some petrol off them. But when his car wouldn't start, he ranted enough to prompt the passers-by to take off. Bremner got angry some more at this, then he lay down by the road and slept.

Meanwhile the Rockhampton police were receiving reports of strange behaviour out in the middle of the

Stretch. They took off for Connors River, and by about 3 a.m. they were clicking handcuffs on Bremner. When asked about his motives, he muttered, 'It must have been my headache.'

dead ends in the bush

Along with the Linfoot story, Bremner's spree had splashed the Horror Stretch into the popular imagination. The stories were spiced with guns, isolation and random fatality, with alcoholic recklessness, rootless victims and perpetrators. People hearing them worried about this anti-Australia where people were worthless, predatory and urgent to be gone.

In many ways the killing of Noel Weckert seemed a species-match with the Linfoot and Robertson cases. But it was especially worrying because Sophie was still missing, and there were no clues identifying the killers. Mystery was piling up. And horror continued to mark the road: on the same day that the *Telegraph* carried its Linfoot retrospective, the Brisbane *Courier-Mail* reported that three travellers had just died in a head-on smash sixty kilometres north of Rockhampton. Either by act of God or act of man, Death was having its way in the brigalow. Also, a 'tropical deluge was hampering search efforts'. The day after Noel's murder, squalls dumped twenty-five centimetres of rain on the

Stretch. The highway was chopped in pieces and torrents surged two metres over the bridges at Connors River and Funnel Creek.

While everyone waited for the waters to subside and for Sophie to turn up, reporters tested each paranoid lead. For example, a story about a hitch-hiker began to pass from newspaper to newspaper. A few days before the Weckert incident, a man had picked up a couple in Rockhampton and driven them to Mackay. When they asked to be set down, the suspect had shoved the man from the car and driven the woman to a deserted siding where he had attempted rape. Quickly the story accrued the right kind of details: police were looking for an escapee from Beaudesert prison outside Brisbane; he was driving a Victorian-registered car which had been stolen some three months earlier in Melbourne. This was perfect. Evil was on the road and it was *from the south*. Old parochial feuds between the Capricornia region and the southern capitals could now add tang to the mystery.

Moreover, the law itself seemed to be contributing to the trouble. An inspector from Brisbane was flying in with five metropolitan detectives who were assigned over a bunch of Mackay detectives and uniformed cops from Marlborough, Sarina, Mackay and Rockhampton. There was a pattern to this administrative move, a pattern that could be traced through decades of secessionist campaigns and intrastate rivalries, not just between Brisbane and Capricornia, but also between the very different philosophies of the Mackay sugar culture and the Rockhampton cattle economy. So in this unruly zone, an old struggle for authority was being replayed around the Weckerts' bodies. Southern law breakers and southern law makers were bringing their customary disruptions.

The metropolitan media began to work the story harder. A week after Noel's murder, the Brisbane *Courier-Mail* front-paged a report about the Beaudesert escapee. He was still at large, and physical and psychological profiles were developing with eye-catching tones: the man was 'jockey-sized' and heavily tattooed; his short hair was 'dyed reddish blond on top' and he was last seen wearing 'a purple suit, with high-heeled brown shoes'. He was like an apparition in a bad dream. Furthermore, an old cell-mate had been interviewed and was warning that 'the man has threatened to shoot it out with police if cornered — he has vowed he won't be taken alive'.

In this atmosphere of amplifying disquiet, the quest continued for Sophie. Who could have taken her? The Brisbane *Telegraph* declared that 'one police theory for the brutality of the crime is that the wanted pair were drug-users'. Most commentators were imagining more than one killer. This meant there was more to worry about than the jockey-sized apparition in the Victorian car. At 4.30 on the morning of the murder, a man who had 'appeared to be nervous' had awakened the proprietor of the Connors River service station and spent five dollars on petrol for an early 1960s model Holden. Another man and possibly a woman were waiting in the Holden. In Wallangarra on the New South Wales border, the tick-gate inspector remembered letting a car like that one through. Also, a 1957 grey-green Holden was being sought. It was carrying three men who were known to be ranging the bush roads from Childers where they had been involved in a robbery and assault two days earlier. The Brisbane *Sunday Mail* gave the particulars:

> The first occupant was about 22 years old, 1.8 m tall wearing a green woollen short-sleeved shirt. The second was an Aborigine about 19, 1.72 m of medium build, with fuzzy hair, many small sores or bites on an arm. The third was about 19, of stocky build, about 1.72 m wearing an army slouch hat, green army shirt, long trousers, and heavy boots with green-edged soles.

Here were wild men, desperate and camouflaged. The country seemed to produce and nurture them. As the *Sunday Mail* reported, police feared that renegades like these could vanish forever via a simple 'detour from the main highway on one of the hundreds of side roads which often lead to dead ends in the bush'. Also the *Courier-Mail* told how police in Darwin had sent their Mackay counterparts the descriptions of six dangerous men who had escaped from the Fanny Bay gaol the previous Christmas, during the epic confusion of Cyclone Tracy. According to badlands logic, these desperadoes would rifle through the Stretch sooner or later.

And still no sign of Sophie. Soon, police were dragging the creeks that flow westward into the inland river systems. The Mackay *Mercury* was getting gloomier: a body gone missing in these circumstances 'could decompose or be lost for years'. Readers were reminded that this was the same country where Ludwig Leichhardt's expedition had disappeared more than a century ago.

Meanwhile, in the absence of anything specific to report about the villains, a picture of the victims was coming together. Noel was thirty-seven, a salesman, the father of two children from a previous marriage. Sophie was a twenty-seven-year-old teacher, a German-born 'New Australian' from Adelaide. They'd met in Whyalla, where Sophie had been teaching and Noel had been odd-jobbing. Deciding to take their chances in North Queensland, they'd enrolled his kids in a Townsville school and begun to build a house in the tropical suburbs. They'd been working their way up towards the good life. It seemed the only risk they ever took was the skydiving.

At last, in the second week of the manhunt, Sophie's body turned up in the scrub that brushed the banks of Funnel Creek thirty kilometres from where Noel had died. A traveller had stepped into the brigalow to piss and had come out puking. Sophie had been shot in the back of the neck, then she'd been broiled by sun, bloated by water and trawled by flood-surges. The local police weren't sure what would give if they tried to move the body, so they stood around waiting for the state health department pathologist to fly in from Brisbane. He would also check for sexual violation. The locals confirmed that the money that had gone missing from the car was not with the corpse.

In newspapers and on television, a speculative intensity leached from the story once Sophie's body had been located. From now on, worst fears and morbid imaginings would be tempered by forensic verification. Also, the jockey-sized man had just been interviewed in Brisbane and he was cleared of suspicion. So the police were under real pressure now. During the days when Sophie was still missing, the case had been a stimulant for the imagination, more fictional than factual. But now the case had to obey the analysis and accountability of law, and the badlands had to transform into the setting for rationale and judgment. So the newspapers began to demand certainties and convictions. The Queensland police minister responded by instructing patrol cars to cruise the highway continuously.

As investigations continued, the unruliness of the road on the night of the killings became more intriguing. Police had compiled a startling list of near-encounters in that desolate place. Two men who had been out pig-shooting recalled that during one late run down the road they had seen a 1964 Holden station wagon, parked and deserted on the roadside, near Funnel Creek at 5.30 a.m. One of the proprietors at the Connors River service station recalled seeing 'something strange' at 3 a.m. when she had heard a disturbance and looked out to watch a Mazda sedan pulling in to the adjoining picnic ground. It was then that she spied a Holden wagon following with its lights off. 'Looking nervous', the Mazda couple had left their car and tried to get into the darkened cafeteria. Finding it locked, they had turned to see the Holden pulling up, still with its lights off. At this tense juncture, a truck had rattled into the picnic area, prompting the Holden to speed off.

Police appealed in vain for the truck driver and the Mazda people to come forward. This stretch of country with so few residents seemed haunted by an ever-growing number of transients. Where fewer than a hundred people lived, up to two thousand people were said to be in daily transit. The harder you looked into this place, the more it seemed to resist a solid definition.

A month after the murders, still no arrest. The *Courier-Mail* reported that in Rockhampton a twenty-six-year-old Aboriginal woman had been sexually tortured and her corpse dumped in the Fitzroy River. Police emphasised that there was no connection with the Weckert case.

At last, on April 12, the Brisbane *Courier-Mail* declared, 'Murder Probe Car Found'. Two men and a woman had been detained by police in Gosford, on the New South Wales central coast, after trying to cash false cheques. They admitted to being on the Rock-hampton-Mackay road at the time of the killing — they had bought petrol at Connors River — and they even claimed to have seen the Weckerts' Celica parked on the roadside, but they swore they had kept travelling south. The Gosford police telexed details to the Brisbane task force, but the Queensland detectives were now concentrating on a differently described Holden, the one the pig-shooters remembered heading *northward* at Funnel Creek. Influenced by a century of regional suspicion, the Queensland detectives distrusted the New South Wales information, so the suspects were not detained in Gosford. Back to zero.

Little mockeries started to irritate the Queensland police now. From Clermont, on the westerly road that connects to the highway near Funnel Creek, a report came in that a man driving a 1964 Holden had held up a farmhouse. A carload of detectives took a couple of days to discover it was a hoax. Also, two New South Wales men claimed to have been woken and stalked by someone driving the Holden after they had fallen asleep beside the road outside Bundaberg, to the south of Rockhampton. Clermont, Bundaberg, Gosford: the trouble was beginning to seep out past the Stretch.

Then success tinged the embarrassment of the authorities: on June 21 the newspapers reported that two men in Goulburn maximum-security gaol were to be charged with the murders. In the recent weeks, seeing no new leads in front of them, the Queensland police had back-tracked through their files and regarded some old things afresh. Weeks before, the men detained by the New South Wales police in Gosford had resumed their scams as soon as the Queensland police said to let them go. Fresh convictions for cheque-fraud, theft and goods-in-possession had kept their files alight, and the Brisbane detectives were relieved to find the men ensconced in the southern system — why not take a closer look at them? (Because they are back in ordinary life nowadays, we'll give them fictitious names: Wilson and Harley.) A six-hour interrogation session in Goulburn jail had rung some bells. Goods were inspected. Ballistics tests were run on a .22 calibre rifle and detectives had flown to Launceston in Tasmania, where the woman who had been seen in the Holden wagon was hiding out. She was extradited, at last, and charged. Seventeen years old, her nickname was 'Gypsy'.

low on everything

The accused were described as itinerant 'roustabouts' and 'sideshow workers', all three originally from Tasmania. Months ago, they'd met at the Goulburn Agricultural Show. One of the men had a car he'd stolen in Melbourne, so they'd decided to go driving. It was quite a jaunt. Gypsy said that 'she could not remember the towns she had been in'. Eventually they hooked up with a fourth Tasmanian drifter who was working the same kind of dodges. They'd got by, pooling resources, siphoning petrol, passing dud cheques, house-breaking and sleeping rough from the Riverina to Cairns and back into New South Wales. A few weeks into the adventure, at Gin Gin in Central Queensland, they'd had good luck and bad. They'd rustled up a .22 calibre rifle during a break-in, but in a stick-up at a service station, the fourth one had been grabbed and the others had taken off south, custodians of the gun.

The night when the remaining three were on the Stretch, they were low on everything — food, petrol, money, good humour. So they decided on some banditry. Lights out, they cruised into Connors River to bleed some fuel from parked cars, but there was a Mazda pulling in just ahead of them and, back up the road, a semi-trailer was changing down through its gears. Plus, someone was sleeping in a ute there. So, amidst all these camp-ground busybodies, they opted for prudence. Waking the proprietor, they spent the last of their money on petrol.

Now they could cruise some more, north for a few minutes, past a Celica parked by the road, back to a roadhouse they'd seen previously. At this sad old cafe, Wilson jemmied his way in, while Harley stayed in the wagon and had sex with the girl. The store yielded no dollars, but there were smokes, some junk food and ammo.

Back on the road, southbound again. This was when they had the idea about the Celica. They checked to see that no headlights were approaching from either direction. Easy money. Wilson got out with the gun and walked over to the driver's side. Noel Weckert woke and refused to cooperate. The court report said he told Wilson 'to go to the shit-house'.

A gunshot chomped Noel's neck. Everything intensified then. Lurching up from the seat alongside Noel, Sophie woke screaming. From the Holden, the other two came running, understanding that the scam had gone out of control. Sophie jagged out of the Celica and was almost collected by a passing car. At least, that was Gypsy's recollection. (The occupants of this car never came forward: more unspecified transients spooking the Stretch.) Gypsy and Harley took off after Sophie. They grabbed and dragged her to the Holden while Noel took a finishing bullet. Wilson came back with money, maybe a hundred dollars.

Knowing they would be heading south eventually, they gunned the car north for thirty minutes, toward Funnel Creek and the Clermont turn-off, thinking this would throw the chase northwest. Sophie was sobbing, Gypsy recalled, so Wilson thumped the hostage as he drove.

The execution happened in a gully. Sophie had fled along the creek-bed as soon as they shoved her out of the car. This last flurry took twenty seconds. Wilson said in court that Sophie was flying, but seeing as how he could knock a bird out of the sky, it was no big chore, hitting her.

A little subdued in the aftermath, they drove south again, past the Celica, over a bridge at Grave Gully, and soon they were spending their new cash on breakfast in a service station at Stockyard Creek seventy kilometres away from the roadblocks. In court, the proprietor recalled that the girl and one of the men were kissing and 'loving up' at the table.

For a few weeks they niggled their way south through New South Wales, beach towns mostly. They swapped the Holden for an old Hillman belonging to the parents of a teenaged hitch-hiker they'd taken home to the river country out back of Lismore. The hitch-hiker had paid with food and a few bouts of sex and then finished the deal by letting the roustabouts sleep on her parents' verandah for a couple of nights. Before long, the killers moved on, running short cons for clean clothes and fried food. Gypsy alternated her nights with each man, the odd one out sleeping under the creaking car.

Finally the boys got taken for shoplifting in some broken town without any street signs. From the Hillman the girl saw them getting into trouble, so she eased the door open and walked to the highway.

Back home in Tasmania, she tried to forget. A few weeks later, Brisbane detectives turned up at her house in Launceston. They sat with cups of tea and just looked at her, as if they knew all about it. So she went talkative. The detectives quietly blessed their dumb luck as they let her tell them everything they didn't know. Next day they were back at the Goulburn jail with extradition orders for the two men.

The trial happened in Mackay in September 1975. Life sentences for the men. Eleven years for the girl. The Brisbane papers concluded it cleanly with condemnations of the killers and muted plaudits for the police. But even as they finished the story, the editorials were keen to keep the country charged up with legend and available for later tales. The *Telegraph* signed off by noting that 'caravaners have returned to camping at night beside the lonely highway', even in the exact spot where the Weckerts had been dispatched.

superimposed scenes

Since following the case in 1975, I've visited the Connors River petrol station and camping-ground several times. Abandoned and vandalised now, it is downright eerie. In this place more quiet than you can imagine, in light harsher and clearer than you want, you stand exposed, running the superimposed scenes in your head. A short history of trouble plays all at once: the Linfoots' caravan rattling past ... Bremner's nights of migraine and rifle practice during the week after he'd bought his gun ... Wilson driving the lights-out Holden into the car park while the Weckerts doze in the Celica just down the road ... a roadhouse proprietor peering through curtains.

The camping-ground was in a sinister state the last time I was there. All around the bullet-pocked petrol bowsers, car bodies were eviscerated in gulches. Middens of 1970s artefacts — Golden Fleece petrol tins, plastic K-tel gadgets, a frisbee chewed by a dog — marked out camp sites that were adorned here and there with more modern relics — a Batman cowl, blue rubber smurfs, a T-shirt printed with Cathy Freeman's smiling face. Realising how recent some of this stuff was, I panned around to see more evidence of current inhabitation. A sleeping-bag and garments were rucked into a corner of the old petrol station office. Broken bottles and thick splashes of blood festooned the dusty slab-floor. Beside an unlocked caravan, a recently used barbeque had been built from car doors.

a pulp history

Standing in the Connors River carpark every few years, conducting my private archaeology of broken things under that witnessing sky, I've come to realise that I've always wanted to know *what* rather than *who* killed Noel and Sophie Weckert. What disturbed and disturbing set of narratives and irresolutions, what mess of fears and desires have generated such debris of violence in the brigalow country? Returning from time to time to skulk around the scene of the Weckerts' execution, I have begun to know their fate as a pulp history of Australia. In their story we learn about the following topics: rootlessness and poverty-struck itinerancy; the imposition of imported law; the geography of vastness, deluge, heat and erosion; the rural culture of firearms; a landscape composed of devolving ecologies; the mind-altering pressures of isolation; nervous, nocturnal predation; prejudice and violence visited upon Aborigines; sex grabbed perfunctorily and illicitly; regionalist resentments; migrations impelled by the shove of hopelessness and bitterness rather than the allure of optimism.

Who in Australia can deny that this litany describes aspects of their local world? Who can honestly say the badlands have nothing to teach them?

There is some spirit of place here, something made by nature and culture scratching a distressed landscape together. It's tempting to take shelter in simplification, to declare that the Horror is just endemic to the Capricorn country, or to insist that the Weckerts were merely caught in some random concussion of fate — something immutable like gravity, and therefore pointless to analyse. We could say it was plain bad luck that all these people with their chancy compulsions came together and behaved the way they did that night in that place. But such a simplification would ignore the fact that human beings make their environments and lay out patterns of expectation, action and reaction there. Truly, the brigalow holds *human* concerns which are historical and therefore mutable. In this landscape, patterns have been worked across space and time by history and by social activity.

Given that human experience arises out of the negotiations between individuals' free will and the larger forces of politics, environment and certain imponderable coincidences, then it was not only fate that grabbed the Weckerts. The Horror they encountered was part of history, something which people set up in barely-known complicity with larger forces such as chance, nature and narrative. This history lives as a presence in the landscape, a presence generated as a forceful outcome of countless actions, wishes and wills — not conscious entirely, not free necessarily. People upon people, land upon landscape. Past upon present and future. This history is facts made by people into stories, rendering events as interpretations, reasons and predictions. History is stories making facts happen. (As Ernst Cassirer explained decades ago, 'in the relation between myth and history, myth proves to be the primary ... factor. It is not by its history that the mythology of a nation is determined but, conversely, its history is determined by its mythology.')

As we dig deeper into the landscape that took the Weckerts, we will uncover many more murder-scenes from the bloody past of Australia's colonial frontier.

HISTORICALLY

Version 4

The Sinister Glamour of Modernity

The colony of Queensland was established just one generation before the 1901 Federation of Australia. Like most colonies it was inaugurated through systematic violence, but atypically its bloody inception is still lodged in recent social memory, in family tales and town litanies that go back just a couple of generations. The Queensland frontier is not radically dissociated from ordinary experience, not relegated safely to some 'ancient' past. In Queensland, colonial times and contemporary times are coeval. This continuity is particularly evident in the Capricorn badlands.

European society was ushered into Central Queensland by a modern force: the Native Police Corps with their mass-produced weapons, their bureaucratic lines of authority and communal actions, their techniques of secrecy and startlingly modern regimes of psychological warfare. Life in Central Queensland today is a *direct continuation* of the systems that formed a new society during the frontier era. And even though most Australians like to believe that 'Queensland is different' (the way Yankees like to dismiss Southerners in the USA), the 'deep north' of Australia can be regarded as a concentrated version of a nation which still prefers to deny the processes that forged it so recently. So, when examining the insistently present past of the Horror Stretch, it is appropriate to begin with a death.

exhumation

On 22 April 1876 a weird case was reported in the *Capricornian* newspaper, published in Central Queensland. Frederick Wheeler, an officer with the Native Mounted Police Force operating out of Belyando Barracks west of the Rockhampton-Mackay track, had just been arraigned and ordered to stand trial for murder. The circuit court had requested the exhumation of the victim, a black stockman named only as Jemmy. This was strange in itself. But even more unusual, the corpse had been buried in a marked grave, European-style — laid to rest in accordance with somebody's idea of respect. Weirder still, a white man had brought charges against Sub-Inspector Wheeler. And the court was taking the case seriously. Bail had been posted and a date set for the trial.

The incident had started innocuously. On 11 March 1876 Wheeler had heard that Jemmy had been loitering with black troopers around the Native Police barracks. Jemmy was popular and affable. Many local whites praised him as reliable. He was employed at the nearby Banchory Station, working stock, and no-one seemed much perturbed about Jemmy's visits to the barracks, except for Sub-Inspector Wheeler. He was incensed twice over, firstly because he believed Jemmy should never have been 'let in' to the European precinct without executive approval, and secondly because an ungoverned black talking with the Aboriginal police might cause his 'tame' ones to slide back. In fact, it later became known that the troopers in Wheeler's contingent had been paying Jemmy to procure women from the local tribe. The frontier was carnal and urgent that way.

The new world that Wheeler inhabited was always poised to tumble out of reason. He never explained this kind of thing to his troopers, but on the evidence of his reports to superiors, he insisted on a scale of human value: at the low rungs, blacktrackers were just above station blacks, who in turn had been raised a little higher than scrub-dwellers. It was Wheeler's burden to maintain the chains of being, to lock them in place. So, with great ardour, he pursued the question of Jemmy's dalliances.

Wheeler was in the habit of 'hauling over' the nearest blacks' camp whenever he learned of misdemeanours in a district. He stoked up to his famous fury, swinging the rifle-butt hard as he prowled the dwellings. It is unclear whether he apprehended Jemmy at the camp or back at the barracks, but some time on March 11 Wheeler ordered his black underlings to truss Jemmy and then throw the long end of rope over the gaol-house rafters. What ensued then, the magistrate was appointed to ascertain.

slips of the pen, marks on the ground

All details of the case would be hearsay, for nothing incriminating about Jemmy's death had been set down on paper. Who had seen the deeds? Black men with no writing, and Wheeler with no intention of writing about this particular incident. Such 'illiteracy' of evidence was the standard Native Police circumstance. By this stage of his career, Wheeler had learned to sweep his report-books clean in anticipation of a paper chase. To this day, he is a ghostly figure in the official records of Queensland. There is no 'character sketch' of him, no 'psychological profile'.

He worked hard to become so unacknowledged. Wheeler (and most of his colleagues in the officer corps of the Native Police) perfected techniques for encrypting great swathes of information about themselves. All over the Central Queensland frontier, strategic terms such as 'dispersal', 'guilt', 'discipline', 'providence' and 'destiny' were thrown up like hessian screens around campaign scenes. For example, after a startling number of Aborigines died while Wheeler was in the Apis Creek district during late September 1872, he filed a report from Marlborough Station explaining that the blacks were dying in great numbers, possibly of poisoning, and that enmity between settlers and natives in the district had become irremediable. Discourse like this implied that the demise of Aboriginality was inevitable and it left the invading militia practically blameless.

Originally known in New South Wales as the Border Police, the troopers were commissioned as up-country boundary riders working to maintain and advance the frontier lines against retaliations by Aboriginal resistance-fighters. In 1842 the Border Police were renamed the Native Mounted Police Corps. Shedding the 'border' reference made sense, because the troopers had begun to push far past the survey lines. In their Queensland campaigns they were fanning out ahead of the squatters who were staking grabs of country to the north. They had become a strike force, riding in squads comprised of six black troopers who were usually governed by two white officers. One or two squads would establish barracks at an outpost and then they would load up munitions and rattle out on patrols lasting from a couple of days to three weeks. More than police, they were the avant garde of cataclysmic change.

The troopers exuded the sinister glamour of modernity. They were equipped with new breech-loading carbines and with horses that were kept fresh and fit in a communication network of well-provisioned stables. The platoons were as fast as they were lethal, gifted with prodigious mechanical and animal advantage over tribal foot-soldiers toting spears. In a world of moral tumult, the troopers — black and white — were free to indulge individualistic appetites as they debased the communal structures of the tribes. This clash of ethics — individual versus communal — defined the frontier. In such a context the word 'dispersal', which was police-report code for 'murder', was actually a clinically accurate description of the troopers' strategy of corroding or dispersing clan solidarity by unleashing the power of each individual trooper's lusts and liberties. Whenever the troopers went into tribal country, they left behind terrible physical damage and immeasurable anger, shame and confusion. On the frontier, the Native Police imbibed whatever they wanted: grog, black women, the astonishing extension of power poised to spring from a loaded gun, the ravenous brigandry of rogue male companionship. For a brief time they were supermen, distance-consuming, machine-strong with personal armament, transcendent of the laws constraining most people (blacks and whites), and therefore they felt unrestrained, beyond good and evil. In short, they were singular modernists, with no allegiance to the past and no responsibility in the present.

---

blacks were set upon blacks

The Aborigines who rode with the platoons were usually recruited in districts distant from the fields they patrolled. This put them in country whose dreaming did not apply to them, meaning they were usually electrified with an intruder's fear at the same time as they were thrilled by a warrior's sense of venture into foreign territory.

Blacks were set upon blacks in a stage-managed, morally chaotic world of border-breach and inter-territorial enmity. Before the European invasion, Aboriginal people had been organised by their country, each tribe sharing a communal consciousness attuned to the needs and demands of the environments which gave them life. It was a system of philosophical, spiritual and nutritional behaviour which might also be described as both an ecology and a legal system. But when Aborigines were recruited into the Native Police, self-satisfaction became the predominant 'ethic'. Blacks and whites now rode carelessly and unlawfully into the tribal country. This word 'self-satisfaction' is crucial. Indulging individualist appetites, the troopers abused the rights and rewards of collective mentalities and they sent the dreamings — the traditional, tribal and ecological forms of consciousness — into disarray. Black strangers thus estranged the world of the Central Queensland tribes. The Native Police were fundamental to the colonists' campaign to destroy pan-Aboriginal morale and to block any cross-tribal solidarity.

hearts and minds

The Native Police were modelled on the paramilitary units that the British had set up elsewhere in their empire. These units always attacked the lands (and therefore the hearts and minds) of the native populations. In India, the British Raj deployed *sepoys* against local communities. There were the *kupapa* regiments in the New Zealand Land Wars, where Maori had been set against Maori as the *pakeha* exploited the intertribal disputes and ambivalences that had existed before the coming of the Britons. Also, the Queensland Native Police inherited some of their rationale from the Irish Police Force. The occupation forces in Ireland were comprised of destitute and demoralised young men sent in from elsewhere in Britain, particularly Scotland, where English colonisation had already triumphed. Australian Aborigines' experiences on the pastoral frontier were similar to the troubles endured by Celtic-speaking Scots when English landlords seized and enclosed traditional lands and then destroyed local ecologies and livelihoods by bringing commercial sheep farming to the highlands. As Henry Reynolds has explained, differences of 'race and culture have for too long obscured the fact that the Aborigines were in a similar situation to those groups in European societies who were being dispossessed and displaced by the penetration of capitalism into traditional rural communities'. Queensland became just one more testing ground for English techniques of industrial takeover.

The pastoral frontier in Central Queensland was greatly influenced by Scottish land-grabbers. It was as if they had learned from the commandeering of their own country and had then applied the bitter lessons in the antipodes. The Archers of Gracemere, the Scotts and Frasers of Hornet Bank, Ross of Keppel Island, Mackay of the Pioneer Valley — so many settlers of Scots heritage paid low wages to displaced Irish peasants to drive sheep and cattle into the Aboriginal territories.

endlessly ponderable

Eventually, force of numbers, disease, new technology, and the Europeans' sense of fated moral preponderance began to wear down the Central Queensland tribes.

But the whites could not have achieved all this on their own. There is no denying that many black people worked in a complicated alliance with the white intruders. Black societies were thus dismantled from inside and out.

The reasons for Aboriginal collaboration with the invaders are daunting to analyse. As are the effects. To borrow Tim Rowse's phrase concerning native-title land claims, the intricacies of frontier power are 'not so much imponderable as endlessly ponderable'. Amidst despair, confusion and intertribal enmity, how might a disarrayed people survive? What is 'right behaviour' in chaos? In times of corporal destruction and spiritual corrosion, the black troops of the Native Police brought a land war to the brigalow, slaying thousands of their 'compatriots'. As the European assaults on the Indigenous world amplified virally, technologically and metaphysically, Aboriginal communities were forced to 'appropriate' new activities and technologies in order to understand, survive and tend the world as it sickened ferociously out of their control. Questions of the 'rightness' and 'wrongness' of every single human action must have been churning up for daily negotiation along the frontier. In this endlessly ponderable context of ethical and ecological mutancy, the Native Police seized their days.

damn the character of the colony

It was apparent to some contemporary observers that the military line of the Central Queensland frontier was also a fault-line of morality. The *North Australian* asserted (on 27 April 1858) that 'the atrocities which [the Native Police] commit, or do not prevent, will damn the character of the colony to all succeeding ages'. Such phrases have reverberated across the decades. We can hear them echo in the language of the High Court's 1992 'Mabo' judgments, as in the report of Justices Deane and Gaudron: 'Dispossession is the darkest aspect of the history of this nation. The nation as a whole must remain diminished unless and until there is an acknowledgment of, and retreat from, those past injustices.' The Mabo judgments are part of a system of moral and legal indebtedness tracing back to the frontier. They acknowledge that although colonialism defined the land as a resource, systems of Aboriginal law have persisted, and this fact makes the country more than a site of economic speculation. The country is thus shaped by persistent obligations, memories and patterns of growth and re-growth. Governed by this system of physical and metaphysical interdependence, the country lives like something with a memory, a force of the past prevailing in the landscape still.

the guilt of others

For Frederick Wheeler though, it was his job to dismember and terrorise and thus to destroy remembrance. There is little *written* evidence concerning him, and he is not easily recalled with conventional historical technique, but he can still be tracked and imagined. Government paperwork concerning Wheeler's early career contains clues dotted like careless drops of blood at a crime scene. Having been appointed second lieutenant of the Native Police in December 1857, Wheeler was involved in campaigns so gory that his entire detachment of twelve troopers deserted. After he was called in to head office to receive the first of several disciplinary tutorials, his commanding officer tabled a tetchy report advising him to temper his zeal. However, this reprimand did not mean he was to desist. Given that the frontier seemed to jag further into wild country as soon as he began his tours, Wheeler developed an ambiguous reputation in government circles. It was not so much his actions that disturbed the administrators. Rather, they worried that *knowledge* of his actions might spread beyond the frontier, back to 'civilisation'. In 1861, in a parliamentary inquiry into the Native Police, he was cited for being too emphatic in the Logan district, where he had lapsed into the habit of neglecting to gather evidence before executing capital punishments. The committee seemed both appalled and impressed: 'Were it not that in other respects he is a most valuable and zealous officer, they would feel it their duty to recommend his dismissal.'

Wheeler's energies scald his early memoranda, for as a young recruit he was proud and declarative of his achievements. Consider his report of October 1858. Wheeler recalls how he had gone out on patrol after hearing that three white men had been slain at Mount Larcombe Station, southeast of Rockhampton. His prose is choppy and menacing like a machete as he remembers riding up to the Calliope River and coming upon a group of forty Aborigines:

> It was too late in the evening to do any good but next morning overtook them but were not able to shoot any as they had already crossed the river. The horses could not gallop in the Mangrove Flats. Only took six or seven gins prisoners. Cannot say whether any of the murderers are amongst the mob, but they must all suffer, for the innocent must be held responsible for the guilt of others as a check on the brutal murders that have just taken place.

Wheeler admits nothing in this narration. Note the absence of first-person pronouns. He does not say 'I did this', perhaps because he feels Destiny acts in him. Or perhaps a man can perform such deeds only by absenting himself from them in remembrance. Wheeler insisted on the blacks being all blood-guilty in the shared degradation of race. Aboriginal suffering was construed as natural and therefore inevitable if the colonists were ever 'to do any good'. Wheeler's daily mission is plain: genocide. But in his own portrayal he is no berserker. Rather, he describes a vocation in the tasks a man tallies before bedding down. He has righteous responsibilities in the chores he must rouse himself to execute early in the morning. Like the sun, he is importunate and unquestionable.

herded into the lake

The most wrathful incident of Wheeler's career may have been the Goulbolba 'dispersal' of 1869. This was relatively late in his career, by which time he had learned to encrypt all written evidence. But even here, account-ability was not erased entirely. He persisted, for example, in oral histories from the white communities in the Nagoa River district west of Rockhampton, as in a report from August 1899, when a correspondent for the Rockhampton *Morning Bulletin* was taken to the Goulbolba site. Walking over the location, a local white man — 'an eye-witness of the battle' — interpreted the place with the following story which the reporter calls a 'traditionary narrative' of the region. The testi-mony can be paraphrased like this:

A white shepherd from St Helen's Station was found speared and mutilated. Recently, the local tribes had been resisting the invasion, and white bodies had been turning up as signs that both sides knew they were at war. But this time, panicky word spread out from St Helen's across the frontier. Stockmen heard that Wheeler's troop had been summoned. They knew he would come in like thunder. One of the station blacks rode out to the camps to warn the clans. Spurred by Wheeler's reputation, the Aborigines went to hide *en masse* in the caves of Goulbolba hill. But they underestimated the Sub-Inspector's tenacity. By dawn the next day, Wheeler had roused the district and assembled an irate force of one hundred whites accompanied by black trackers who followed spoors to the cave-pocked hill. Later in the day, by the time the troopers rode back to their barracks, three hundred Aborigines — men, women and children — had been shot dead or herded into the lake for drowning.

They must have all suffered. It was said that for thirty years the lakeshore and hillside were white with bones, until a bushfire cremated the site in 1898.

stories placed in the landscape

'Hard' evidence of this massacre — in the form of court transcripts, photographs, police reports, archaeological relics, or notarised contemporary testimonials — is unavailable. Absences like these bedevil all research into Australian frontier history. But, 'unreliable' as it is as conventional history, the Goulbolba tale is significant because it is so generic. All over the Australian frontier, stories like it have been placed in the landscape. Outside of Bathurst. Near Yeppoon. On the Moree plains. In Tenterfield. The set-up is the same in each case: a sentinel landform — a hill, a ridge, a rocky outcrop — looms over a flat tract of country that has been hit by more violence than is immediately evident. Sighting the sentinel, a storyteller is prompted into narration. The landscape itself has a memory, and the storyteller activates it so that the community can know its place in the world of time and space.

Sceptics can object that these slaughter accounts are merely yarns passed around without proof. But this ignores how seriously oral cultures (white as well as black) regard their environments and their narratives. Cultures which do not rely on written records know that their environment is their world of meaning, because landmarks hold the prompts to the stories that constitute knowledge. In such cultures only a fool would be careless with narrative, for to have no care about the stories of your setting is to nullify your life in the place that determines your survival. The Goulbolba story is generic because Native Police techniques were generic. Habitually, troopers found the ideal locations for their work. The massacre sites were on the outskirts of settlements, where the new technologies of horse and rifle could overcome the traditional practice of high-ground vantage. In traditional Aboriginal techniques of battle it was probably always prudent to have the protection of a known landmass at your back. But as soon as guns were involved, this old wisdom could be baffled — at the back of a canyon or against a granite bluff, away from the scrutiny of the township, the troopers could herd and cull the natives without coming within range of spears.

The Goulbolba legend has mythological force. Which is not to say it is false. The narrative cannot be dismissed as fantasy, especially when it is considered in the context of the undeniable damage that Wheeler inflicted elsewhere. True, there are dubious elements to the story, such as the fire that conveniently eliminated material proof of the massacre. But to disregard the account is to misunderstand how communal narrative works. The fire is included in the story because it gives listeners a palpable sense of the secrecy, frustration and disappearance that must be *felt and known* to be part of frontier history. This is a story told to provide a disturbing model of the events that have shaped everyday consciousness in the colonial landscape. A forceful story will *evoke* as well as record what happened, offering a version of colonial experience including the *structures of feeling* that settled into the social environment. Secrecy, ambiguity and inconclusiveness are part of what happened — so the story must figure these experiences in the listener's thoughts and feelings. A forceful story will conjure these feelings in a communal consciousness, a dramatic union of speakers and listeners. The Goulbolba tale has such force.

the way a frontiersman's blood flowed

It is a hard, irrefutable fact that the tribes of Central Queensland were disintegrated in a cataclysmically short period of time. Massacres as large as the Goulbolba slaughter must be factored in to the history of the region. Around nearby Halifax Bay, for example, the black population was estimated at more than five hundred in 1865; fifteen years later there were twenty-two people left. And in Mackay, the four great tribes of the river country lost half their people within eight years of white incursion. Officers like Frederick Wheeler saw it all happen. Modernists that they were, they indulged themselves in mechanical power and the disintegration of communal strength, and they *made it all happen.*

How can we know Frederick Wheeler today? How did this ungovernable man simultaneously shape and conceal the colonial world that produced the contemporary world? Imagining out from the written smatterings and legends of his deeds, we must suppose Wheeler had a plan. When he exerted himself so prodigiously at Goulbolba, for example, his actions must have been founded on a rationale. He must have believed in whiteness, in the preponderance of light-filled, abstract thought governing the darker forces of action and reflex. Though he never would have declared himself one, he must have been an early example of the social Darwinist, someone convinced that nature and history were working together to make manifest the destiny of white men. The fact that Wheeler worked so hard for twenty years suggests that he had his personally justified understanding of colonial order. Bloodlust could not have sustained itself so long unless it was supported by theories and belief.

words and deeds

Moreover, once an officer became as zealous as Wheeler, the corps worked out ways to cosset him. They avoided muzzling him in the field so long as he learned how to re-present his achievements unimpeachably on paper.

But why were the lieutenants required to write reports at all? This seems puzzling at first, for writing constitutes evidence and therefore produces the stray chance of culpability. True. But the writing fulfilled at least two purposes. First, it was a ritual of governmental accountability, a means of ritualising and 'realising' the new European order. The reception and tabling of reports and inquiries about the Native Police were ceremonies marking the transition of frontier country into law. The writing worked on the country, rendering it a known quantity. Secondly, within the more intimate and immediate confines of camps and barracks, the reports asserted a difference between white officers and black troopers. To write a report was a performance that showed whites and blacks who was who on the great chain of being.

Officers were taught to avoid reaching for the pen the way they reached for the carbine, with their blood up. And what guns they took up! The munitions manufacturers Snider & Co. knew about words and blood. The company had a motto for the colonial market: 'A Snider is a splendid Civiliser'. The .577 inch breechload carbine that the company sold during the early 1870s was portable apocalypse. It could be loaded quickly and repeatedly, even on horseback, and it discharged a soft lead ball the size of a cherry. When the ball hit bone, it spread into a scouring disc that tore a ragged hole through a body. The carbine was not especially accurate, but at close quarters, or in a horseback pursuit, a couple of shots could chop a man into irregular pieces. Along with the Martini-Henry Mark II .450 inch rifle, the Snider was the main machine that broke the Central Queensland frontier during the 1860s and 1870s, after the black resistance had held firm against older firearms.

At the 1858 Select Committee Inquiry into the Native Police, William Archer of Gracemere declared that he was appreciative of the work the troopers were doing on his behalf and if the Native Police Corps did not exist, frontiersmen would have invented them by organising their own vigilante cavalries. But he must have known that pastoralists could not have been so swift and efficient in their executions. Also, if the corps did not exist, the pastoralists would have been obliged to confront their own blood-guilt far more directly than actually happened wherever the 'savage' troopers did the bloodletting for them.

This is how the gun and the pen took the country. Indulging themselves in the field and governing themselves in their reports, the white officers of the Native Police jinked a two-step of violent action and circumspect remembrance. They wrapped their deeds in dissembling verbiage and eventually they became their own twisted idioms, developing a 'pathological' disconnection between doing and declaring, a disconnection which gave them no way to see the world clearly, no way to analyse and comprehend the changes that were coming toward them.

The troopers were unprepared to adapt to the new requirements that civilians brought to the country once the frontier wars waned. The Native Police were not required to settle on the ground they sullied. By venting their violence and then moving on, the troopers shielded civilised people from the knowledge that murder and undeclared war were the reasons they 'owned' their land. The corpsmen were encouraged to act as if memory was irrelevant to them.

Which is why Frederick Wheeler must have been greatly puzzled to find that, in 1876, he was being called to account for the death of Jemmy of Banchory whom he knew, in his own mind, to be worth no remembrance.

At the Belyando Barracks on 11 March 1876, Wheeler had ordered his blacks to string Jemmy up by the heels. He demanded they whip the prisoner. Then he stepped in for the type of performance that seems to have been his hallmark. He showed his charges just who was capable of everything, from abstract instruction through to concrete destruction. Shoving the blacks aside, Wheeler dropped Jemmy to the floor and asserted himself with kicking.

Robert McGavin, master of Banchory, found Jemmy in time to watch him die, out near the blacks' camp. The haemorrhages took days to finish him, blood festering where Wheeler's boots had branded him. After burying the corpse, McGavin headed for the nearest magistrate. Even in death, therefore, Jemmy got hauled further away from the Aboriginal world, into the funerary habits and laws and legacies of whiteness as the colonial world shifted its patterns of governance.

What was McGavin doing, pressing charges against Wheeler? Perhaps he was outraged that another man had so disabled his investment. Perhaps he was asserting his sovereignty as a pastoralist over the troopers who continued to presume they could range unencumbered wherever they wanted. Or perhaps he was a decent man moved to seek something like justice.

There is evidence in settlers' journals and letters that hatred of the Native Police invariably brewed amongst white communities once the frontier had moved on and the settler-outposts were beginning to regard themselves as civic hamlets. Some white land-grabbers in Central Queensland did attempt ceremonies of negotiation between themselves and the station blacks. This is not to imply that justice was common in the cross-cultural transactions that occurred in the aftershock of the land wars. Any civility in interracial relationships was *allowed* by the victors rather than *accorded*, one to the other, by free subjects who were equally powerful. Even so, there were some landholders who, through pragmatism most frequently, were attempting to establish protocols of mannerly exchange with blacks on their properties. For example, in 1862 Charles and Henry Dutton of Albinia Downs station waged a letter-campaign in the *Sydney Morning Herald* and the *Rockhampton Bulletin*, trying to prevent the Native Police from riding onto the property and interfering with newly established routines of co-tenancy with the local blacks. The troopers refused to allow stable relationships of any kind between whites and blacks, and the Duttons wanted to replace this rule of intimidation. They were hoping for an easier style of hegemony, something self-sustaining where the various classes felt the system of power to be procedural and inevitable rather than forcibly and endlessly asserted. Most likely, at Banchory, Robert McGavin was of similar mind.

---

settlement time

In a blow, the Native Police could destroy a settler's strategies of truce and accommodation. Once the land-grabbing was done, the Native Police were useful only for bearing the blame for the bloodshed of colonial expansion. For a short time after they had completed their work as shock-troopers, they were usually required as scapegoats. By the mid-1870s, however, many whites were arguing that the Native Police had become an *impediment* to security and wealth. No longer did set-tlers value the brigandry of the troopers. Ironically, characters such as Wheeler were now seen as too savage. He fell foul of the settlers' desires for legitimacy as the Native Police were now seen as vestiges of the 'discovery years'. The troopers did their job so thoroughly they made themselves redundant.

It is not so strange, then, that the magistrates seized on the 1876 Banchory case and took the opportunity to define Frederick Wheeler as a criminal: here was a chance to take the rogue out of the field and to pretend that settlement had been achieved. But the authorities never planned to incarcerate him, they just wanted him gone. Magistrate John Murray, formerly an inspector with the Native Police, heard the arraignment and set the trial for October 2 — six months away — tacitly granting Wheeler ample time to organise his own disappearance.

Magistrate Murray knew well how this shape-shifting worked. Not long ago he had managed to reinvent himself and find a place in the post-frontier world. Murray's epiphany had come in 1860 when he had been in command of a troop which was tried for the murder of a white woman.

so much death cannot be traceless

This is what had given Murray such a fright when he was in uniform, a sudden bout of violence almost swallowed him despite his attentiveness. A young woman named Briggs received the first blow. A tavern worker at the Old Royal Hotel in Sydney, Fanny had ventured north in 1860. On the ship out of Brisbane she met a Rockhampton settler named Johnny Watt and they disembarked together at the Fitzroy River wharf to set up house just outside town. On 6 November Watt was attending to his new business venture, a butcher shop in the high street. When he returned home, Fanny was gone. The Native Police were called, but a laborious search failed to locate any tracks. Townspeople joined in. Other blacktrackers were summoned from the southern districts. Everyone was puzzled to see how the local troopers had overlooked some obvious spoors. When the violated body was found flyblown, the townsfolk were both irate and terrified.

Suspicion fixed on the local troopers, for they had opportunity, motive and habitual patterns. As a colonist reminisced years later, settlers were always disturbed to see that the Native Police were 'fond of roaming about in the woods' whenever they were recuperating at the barracks after weeks of patrolling. Presently, on the evidence of some fringe-dwelling blacks who had been plied with drink and threats, four of the local black troopers — Gulliver, Toby, Johnny Reid and Alma — were arrested. An Aboriginal woman who had previously been maltreated by the troopers was put up to tell how these four had encountered 'the white Mary' in the scrub when Fanny was looking for some of Watt's stray horses.

This crime, enacted in the bush on the edge of the law, allegedly perpetrated by men undefined by the law, was judged and punished as the law turned aside: Gulliver was 'shot while attempting to escape' after the white troopers had told him to start running; Toby was taken out into the bush, where he 'died from fever' and was put in a shallow grave; Alma was 'shot while attempting to escape' when he was taken to the river to collect water for the barracks. Curiously, Johnny Reid was granted a fearful freedom. Perhaps John Murray kept him alive as a permanent, terrified advertisement for the power of police judgment. And perhaps this was the point of refusal, where Murray took himself over to the judiciary.

The most disturbing aspect of the Fanny Briggs case was the way it suggested that *no-one*, not even the officers of the corps, ever really knew what the platoons were up to. Murray saw how public sentiment was shifting, now that white women and children were arriving in the settlements and the unaccountability of the Native Police added up to fear and insecurity in the hamlets rather than effectiveness on the frontier.

John Murray saw new laws emerging to constrain his roistering world and he understood that it would become evermore governed. So he insinuated himself into the magistracy. When the case of Jemmy turned up, Frederick Wheeler must have appeared to Murray like a sign of how bad Murray himself could have gone, had he been unable to analyse the new dynamics entering the colony those few years earlier. As for Wheeler, he was the flint of violence, in no way malleable. An absolutist who had grown accustomed to living unregulated, Wheeler was unprepared for change. In being so single-minded, he failed to look up and see how the wider world had altered around him.

On 3 October 1876, six months after Murray had processed Wheeler at the preliminary hearing in the case of Jemmy of Banchory, the *Rockhampton Bulletin* noted that the accused had not presented for his full trial now that the circuit court had returned. Wheeler never turns up again in any Australian records. The mode of change he represented — his violent avant gardism — was no longer desirable in a world that was settling into the conservative patterns that would be required by the new Federation, this White Australia.

the resumption of life

The troopers had developed a crazy ability to slaughter and simultaneously to deny all knowledge of what they were committing. The corpsmen had been daubing themselves in blood and carrying on as if they were clean. In existentialist parlance, this is the maddening vertigo of 'bad faith'. Or, to think in Freudian metaphors, such duplicity must lead eventually to a thunderous return of the repressed, given that the trauma of participating in so much death cannot be traceless, no matter how avidly one attempts to turn away from what happened. When people deliberately vent so much blood and then refuse to acknowledge the gore, they are likely to be pursued by guilt and grief so long as the trauma is ignored rather than acknowledged. The same goes for people who *commission* the bloodletting — as the colonist did with the troopers — in the hope that they will not to have to witness it. Remembrance worries away at repression. If there are any survivors, or even if there are merely witnesses, in the aftermath of an attempted genocide, murder bleeds through stories via memory. Victims and victors — both can't help but remember.

How can a society own up to the debts of remembrance? In Michael Lesy's *The Forbidden Zone* — an unsettling study of North American mortuary rituals — a funeral director is quoted pondering the purpose of his work. He refers to personal grief, but his thoughts can also apply to the afflictions and needs of any nation that has to confront the legacies of colonialism:

What we're responsible for, beyond the physical facts of simple removal, preparation, and deposition, is orchestrating the ritual of grief, the process of mourning, the rite of passage that begins at the moment of death. We help people understand that the person who was living is now a person who is dead. My motto is 'See, Touch, Feel, and Believe.' You *see* the dead; you *touch* the dead. The evidence of your senses impels you to *feel* grief. Grief, anger, sorrow, loss. Those *feelings*, provoked by the senses, lead you to the *belief* that what was is no longer. Without that belief, no one can resume their own life. The resumption of life is the goal of all mourning.

speak with the dead

With the mourning that he ministers, the funeral director undertakes a vocation strikingly similar to an historian's responsibility. This is an idea proffered by Stephen Greenblatt, in a personal memory when he recalls the lugubrious men who offered their services at the gates of the Jewish cemetery in Boston, the city of his childhood. Greenblatt remembers how these daunting characters were paid to put on a display of grief, to make the fact of loss and change seem mundane and somehow controllable so that the bereaved visitors might commence the pragmatic routines of resuming life. The professional mourners waited at the gates and offered their services to grief-stalled people, prompting the sufferers into the dynamics of exchange, taking money to give change so that some mortally disagreeable facts of life could be transformed in something ordinary and negotiable. Historians, composing their stories and putting communal memories on display, are similar figures, ministering small ceremonies of mourning, transaction and resolution.

Elsewhere, Greenblatt explains his vocation as an historian: 'I began with the desire to speak with the dead,' for the dead have 'contrived to leave textual traces of themselves, and those traces make themselves heard in the voices of the living.' The historian strives to amplify and translate these voices, in the hope that the dead will settle and allow present communities to live peaceably once the past has been acknowledged and made palpable in the public domain. And because the dead persist in the stories which the living use to represent existence to themselves, the dead always need to be felt and believed through storytelling and ritual so that the living might be informed by the past rather than be haunted and paralysed by it.

Sooner or later, any society that would like to know itself as 'post-colonial' must confront an inevitable question: how to live with collective memories of theft and murder? Sooner or later, therefore, acknowledgment and grieving must commence before healing can ensue, before the badlands can be understood as redundant.

Not long after the Native Police left thousands dead and unburied in the Queensland brigalow country, newcomers tramped in. With no professional mourners to help them live on this funeral-ground, the settlers tried to regard the place as new and unstained, as if there was nothing residual to see, touch, feel and believe. But they were overwhelmed by the fact that death had been recently and prodigiously abroad. Fear and denial have ghosted Queensland ever since. In April 1876, for example, the editor of the *Brisbane Courier* tried to clear his mind when he read the news of Frederick Wheeler's impending trial:

> If the Aborigines were more civilised than they are, we should either make treaties with them or we should be at open war with them. It would then be either peace

or war on certain terms, and we should be guided by the principles of action recognised in such cases.

It's striking how pertinent his confusion and candour remain today, in this society that continues to yearn for the disappearance of its founding traumas.

To be rid of these traumas, we need to imagine how to transcend the cruelty that seems to have defined colonialism. To do so we need imagination in the present day but also advice from the past, in case there were characters and scenarios that were already working against the badness that was seeping into the land. Past characters and scenarios that might teach us something now. The story of James Morrill, in the next version, is a case in point.

Version 5

A History of Quiet Suspicion

In 1863 a blackened man hailed some settlers outside Port Denison, just to the north of the brigalow country. He signalled them not to shoot and then stuttered words that are still famous: 'I am British object.'

This was James Morrill. He has caught the attention of several writers through the decades, most famously David Malouf in his novel *Remembering Babylon*, for Morrill seems to have brought something, some quality, back with him. What did he have for us? What kind of omen was he?

Haltingly in front of the gunmen, the apparition remembered his European name and how to form the guttural grammar of English. Recalling that he had been shipwrecked on the Great Barrier Reef, he offered a few images that he'd carried long and privately: how the first mate had clambered into a lifeboat panickily carrying nothing more than a live sheep — the beast and the man drifting away from the rest of the party in the other boat, the man realising too late that he had no sail, no oar, no rudder; how Morrill and the ship's captain had caught a shark with the severed limb of a starved companion — the monster swimming through a loop of rope at the instant it seized the great morsel; how a man called Wilmot had watched his wife die in his lap, after which he had undressed her and tipped her overboard, where the body floated whitely alongside the boat for twenty minutes until she sank unmolested amidst the circling fish; how the captain had carved forty-two day-notches on the gunwales before the boat drifted onto a mainland beach. Morrill remembered stumbling through the hinterland for a fortnight, weakening to hallucination all the while, watching Wilmot and another man lie down and die, until a group of Aborigines finally came with food and shelter. Morrill thanked them by singing a hymn, 'God Moves in a Mysterious Way'.

research the interloper

Since then, he had spent seventeen years living with different tribes in North Queensland. In the company of his hosts he had learned several languages, travelled thousands of miles and met innumerable black people.

In both worlds — Aboriginal and European — the hubbub around this 'wild white man' was intense. Even as he was now becoming a celebrity among Port Denison's gentry, Morrill could remember how, seventeen years earlier, he had also been an object of research and contention among the black people. In a transcript of his reminiscence, published not long after his return, he explained that during the first year of his Aboriginal life (1846) he had been the keynote topic of a great symposium of black people:

> Time ran on and the natives began to collect in great numbers — we knew them to be strange … When they all arrived, they numbered considerably over a thousand souls … they belonged to about ten different tribes. We learned that some of the tribes belonged to the country far south of where we were.

Morrill realised that the Aborigines had congregated to debate him, to research an interloper and compare his characteristics with all the 'intelligence' that was already circulating concerning the white invaders from the south.

Telling his story to the citizens of Port Denison a generation later, Morrill recalled how the symposium had passed without incident and the seasons rolled by as he participated in vast treks to visit and barter with faraway peoples. It is not clear whether he attended the conference of feasting and confabulation that occurred every three years in the Bunya Mountains, south of the Horror Stretch, where thousands of Aborigines from all over southern and central Queensland used to gather to grow fat on pine nuts while exchanging information and goods. But he must have met many people who had been 'delegates' there. And they would have told him stories from even farther afield.

Morrill's account and similar stories of Aboriginal cosmopolitanism and cohesion circulated throughout the colony. They contradicted any simple myth of European triumph. In this place and time when most people knew that the blacks were organised and knew also how much violent dispersal had been required to establish white settlements in Aboriginal country Australia-wide, Morrill was a reminder to be chary of tales that portrayed European settlement as natural, inevitable or predestined. The fact was, there remained a cogent confederacy of Aboriginal intelligence all across Australia, even in the places the colonists liked to imagine as blank and unmanageable.

Huge portions of Australia were attuned to each other at Aboriginal conferences. For example, the nations of the granite-belt to the west and south of Toowoomba, the river people of northern New South Wales, the tribes from the acacia country around the Dawson River: they all seem to have been regular participants at the Bunyah Mountain gatherings. They would have shared their information with the more northerly tribes whenever encounters occurred in journeys during the three years between conferences.

Through such systems of trekking, Indigenous communities circulated commodities, ideas and warnings across enormous distances. And it was obvious to James Morrill that he had become part of a trade network, that he was a token in Aboriginal currency. He said it out loud: 'I am British object.'

---

the law of the world

Now this man, who was somehow black as well as white, had come back to the colonists. Mayors and councillors invited him to dine, newspapermen came with quills in hand, women pointed and spoke in low tones. Morrill endured this for a few days, and then hiked out to sit down one last time with his adoptive tribe:

> I told them the white men had come to take their land away. They always understand that might not right is the law of the world, but they told me to ask the white man to let them have all the ground to the north of the Burdekin, and to let them fish in the rivers; also the low grounds they live on to get the roots — ground which is no good to white people, near the sea-coast and swampy.

As it turned out, Morrill misjudged the settlers attitudes about the coastal country. Perhaps he had been away from colonists too long. The low grounds may have been no good for sheep and cattle, but the white people set great strategic value on *all* waterways. Seizing them had become a standard tactic worldwide: by securing the rivers, the spiritual and victual pulse of the original occupants could be subdued. Moreover, the black people of Queensland had not yet seen industrial agriculture. Nor had Morrill, probably. They could not have known that in the tropics the settlers were beginning to invest in a special crop. Sheep and cattle would rot in the humid paddocks, but sugar could thrive there.

So, in the coastal tracts at the northern end of the brigalow country, contact between Aborigines and newcomers was soon governed by the rituals and seasonal timescales of plantation life, just as station life ruled in the southern cattle-country. After the brutish and short encounters with the Native Police who had preceded the settlers, the surviving Aborigines now engaged with pastoralists and farmers in a more 'involving' set of relations and exploitations. Blacks and whites began to encounter each other habitually, in workaday ways. Native and newcomer meshed incrementally into each other's hearts and minds, at locations like camp sites, watering holes, harvest fields, stockyards and scrub-clearance tracts — wherever meetings took place repeatedly and vocationally rather than spasmodically and belligerently.

This slow, scouring process is how settlements were established all over Australia, but especially in Central

Queensland. People from districts north of the Brisbane River have always known that there is no singular story of settlement, no decisive myth that can portray the accession of European power as 'natural' and complete. Almost everyone involved with European settlement in Central Queensland knew that factionalism, coercion and irresolution defined colonial life. If a myth can be understood as a neatly resolved story that we tell ourselves so that we are not paralysed by the contradictions in actual experience, then the land-grabbing and settlement of Central Queensland could not be described (at the time) or remembered (by inheritors) with a persuasive myth. Too many people knew that the lands had been seized in unforgettable ways that were less than heroic.

So, unable to celebrate simple, righteous sovereignty in their new locale, the settlers of the Capricorn hinterland stayed quiet. This is how the badlands lodged in the colonial mentality. All over frontier Queensland, settlers drew reticence closely around themselves. In newspapers and journals from this time there are compacted stories and letters terse with anxiety, indignation and hints of dreadful anticipation. There is not much crowing or self-congratulation. And this sensibility has been transmitted through the generations.

some deep stun

For example, consider the *fin-de-siecle* era, the time approaching 1900. We might expect to find an effervescent mood as the colony moved toward national Federation. But in Central Queensland (and doubtless in many other parts of the inchoate nation) a kind of communal neurosis gripped the white population. Photographic portraits from these times witness it with shocking candour, for the camera was still unfamiliar and people had not yet learned to mask the emotions that set their nerves and muscles ajangle in front of the deadpan lens. The photographs show faces forced awry by spiritual strain. Many of these people had seen too much violence during the frontier days and it disturbed them to their souls.

Disturbance in the soul is perhaps more prosaically understood as persistence in the memory. To say it simply, many white inheritors and most black survivors of the frontier were unable to forget the violence that produced the riches of the burgeoning nation. Discomforted by easy stories of their righteousness in the new settlements, these people were looking into the future, their expressions dark with an inarticulate malaise. No matter how much self-conviction or arrogance sheened the faces, many of them were also taut with some deep stun of alienation and doubt. Here were people unimaginably tough and undeniably brittle. Determined, yet also haunted somehow.

All along the Queensland coast, photographers snared portraits in nervy enclaves of white people who perceived themselves to be suspended in savagery. Acting on the information released by the first land-claimers, settlers had come prying in ships or on bullock drays and then they had hunkered down and fortified themselves against the outnumbering natives. Those who had pitched the first tents and kept watch soon found that this was not earth for easy inheritance. Often, by the time the livestock and new citizens arrived, the vanguard communities had failed to feel any encouragement in the landscape and they were ailing spiritually.

This is not to disparage the settlers. They had extraordinary qualities. Their stoicism, for example. The perseverance that is required to farm the tropical bush takes some effort even to imagine. The scrub appears endless. So do heat and lassitude. Doggedness seems the only emotion worth entertaining, as trees must be taken out singly and slowly, to clear stock-runs or paddocks for planting. If one's mind starts to range for variety, it may never come back.

All this accounts for the generic Central Queensland face that takes shape in every generation of settler-descendants. A cast gets set on European visages that have worked too hard outdoors for too long. A landscape unto itself, this face can still be seen today in pubs and diners, in the cabs of trucks. The mouth is a serrated horizon-line. Furrows mark a neck and jaw-line champed to the rigours of adversity. Eyes are tarped with forebearance. When one encounters the face in bus stations and roadhouses, it is usually not reading or talking. It is persisting, wasting no vigour, wisely, and keeping to itself whatever it knows. It's the right kind of countenance for contemplating the brigalow, and it first took shape during the settlement years. It is in hundreds of photographs from the late-nineteenth century. Deep disquiet lurks in pictures of wedding guests, in the regard of missionaries, prospectors and gaolers. No matter how fervidly they might have told themselves the land was there for the taking, many of these people knew in their souls that they were not getting anything for free.

I look at these old photographed faces now, so similar to many that I grew up with (in fact it is the kind of face that I often notice myself wearing) and I see a regional 'affliction'. Or, to say it less pejoratively, I see history. I see an unease shaped out of the original settlers' almost obsessive suspicion of permeable boundaries, around stockyards and homesteads, most literally, but also around philosophical categories in this place where the Europeans' definitions and pre-sumptions were often perturbed by the knowledge that they were interlopers and that there was much that they had yet to categorise and comprehend. For to live as a new settler in this place was to be in a quandary.

How to recognise everyday events and objects as signs? What to make of the Aborigines' demeanour? How to 'read' the weather, the skittish behaviour of stock, the ailing and blooming of fodder?

With such questions pressing in, some settlers grew evermore tormented as they witnessed the degree of violence and vigilance required not only to usher in but also to maintain the European way of life. Tetchy letters, and the occasional aghast one, about trigger-happy boundary riders and station managers were sent by new farmers to local newspapers and to Brisbane and Sydney journals. Clearly, many colonists were disturbed by their post-frontier life.

There were other types of written accounts, too, which told less explicitly, but no less effectively, of the tensions and deep anxieties in the new colonies. The exploration journal of a settler named John Mackay is a case in point. It is an ordinary tale of speculation and adventure that, on first glance, seems to be about a successful frontier venture but ultimately it leaves the reader with an abiding sense of Mackay's failure to recognise and reconcile the liabilities that get established when theft is the basis of burgeoning prosperity. Without intending it, the ambitious young Scotsman shows how silence, suspicion and dissembling are the legacies of colonialism. His story needs a few pages of preamble before we get to its revelations.

the meaning of the white men

In 1860 John Mackay took a posse of land-selectors north from Marlborough Station near Rockhampton. At the end of the first day, Mackay opened his journal and set the tone for the rest of the expedition:

> At sundown we camped on a creek running to the S.W., and while preparing supper were surprised by about a dozen of the natives, well armed, appearing on the opposite of the creek, and, fearing others might be in the vicinity, Robinson fired over their heads, when they fled down the creek.

This may have been the first of millions of gunshots soaked up by the brigalow around the Tropic of Capricorn. Perhaps both factions already knew that conflict rather than consultation was the meaning of the white men. Perhaps neither group felt any need or hope for translation and conciliation. Whatever the preconceptions, once the gun was fired the Aborigines decided to track the visitors at a distance, keeping them under quiet observation at all times and handing them on to the next relevant group whenever the trek came to the edge of custodial territory.

Mackay's men meandered with the Isaacs River as it insinuated the rainshadow behind the coastal range. The party's sightings of Aborigines travelling with tools and hunting booty indicate that this was a traditional trekking route. Given that the track (which nowadays is paved and known as a portion of National Highway One) carried such traffic, there must have been songs, names, dances and body markings that held the knowledge needed for travelling well in this country. Native rituals and laws must have kept the place lively in the consciousness of the five or six thousand black people estimated to have been living in the 'Port Curtis and Leichhardt Pastoral Districts' before the white people came. But for the new settlers, the brigalow basin was a hard land to bring immediately into the colonial dream of pasture and providence.

the meaning of the brigalow

Whatever the flood plains of Central Queensland meant in Indigenous lore, the first Europeans had no deep affinity for the country. Mackay complained of 'one immense scrub'. He lingered atop the range north of Marlborough and then he and his entourage waded single-file into the acacia, quickly feeling unsettled in this place where they lost the vista and had to rely mostly on noise and smell for their ways of orienting themselves. Many visitors to the brigalow — sniper victims most notably — have described their panic when they realised how tightly their vision was hemmed by the scrub. This 'blindness' must have been particularly distressing to explorers who yearned for extensive prospects to survey and claim. They were literally looking for a place where their landowning destiny was manifest in front of them, but contained by the brigalow they were the opposite of sovereign subjects, they were like objects governed by an overwhelming power. As one old frontier veteran explained to the 1861 Parliamentary Inquiry into the Native Police, 'You go into the scrub, the blacks are all around you, and you can see nothing of them.' Here was country for European *un*settlement.

In this bush 'infested by blacks', Mackay and his companions endured numbing, unvarying hours:

> To-day we began our northward journey along the valley of the river, a recital of which would prove but of little interest, each days' [sic] experience being so similar in incident, such as cutting our way through dense scrub, swimming creeks, etc.

But variety would burst out occasionally:

> About noon a large party of natives crossed ahead of us on a small plain, when having gained the edge of the scrub, they sent the women and children away, remaining themselves, with the apparent intention of stopping our further progress. Rounding the pack-horses up, Macrossan, Duke and I went towards them, when one of them, suddenly darting out on the plain, hurled a spear in the direction in which Duke was approaching, which fortunately fell short of the mark. We at once fired over their heads, when they disappeared in the scrub, leaving their war implements and a net containing some fish and a

large iguana. Taking the fish we left in payment a toma-hawk, a sheath knife and a pumpkin.

Possibly, the spear-throwing was not an attack so much as a ritualistic invitation to negotiate fair passage. Duke was an Aboriginal guide whom Mackay had employed on the way up from northern New South Wales. Notably, the spear was thrown toward the only black man in the group of intruders. It may have been 'offered' as a sign, a cue to commence a meaningful exchange. Perhaps it was part of the technology of Aboriginal communication. Duke may have been ex-pected to return an appropriate object or gesture. But without the patience, grammar or security to perceive this thing 'linguistically', the Europeans seem to have made a categorical misinterpretation and responded as if the spear was principally belligerent rather than lexi-cal. The white men took no time to hear an interpre-tation of the event from Duke. Gunfire was their prompt reply. A sign was received as a weapon and a different weapon was sent back, which the Aborigines received as a sign. Transmitted through the confusion, one message was plain enough: enmity rather than interaction was intended by the whites. So the blacks kept their silence and withdrew into the brigalow.

Mackay notes that he took to aiming his rifle pro-gressively lower whenever Aborigines approached. But he mentions no deaths other than Duke, who wasted away with a puzzling ailment which may have been malaria but may also have been a kind of soul-sickness exacerbated by his sense of intrusion in other Aborigines' territory. On 13 June one of Mackay's party, Andrew Murray, noted that 'Duke was very poorly and seemed quite without heart'. The white men were powerless to encourage him, and soon afterwards he was buried in a shallow grave near Funnel Creek, just a gunshot away from where Sophie Weckert's body would be found more than a century later.

After the burial, Mackay persevered north, arriving at a river which he named after himself. (It was later gazetted as the 'Pioneer' by the office of Crown Lands Regulation.) This watercourse was the prize he was looking for. Now he could return to civilisation to stock up and formalise his land-claim.

grief plus ire

From this moment on, they were in competition with time, to beat other squatters out there surveying for new property. Hurrying back to Rockhampton, Mackay and his companions succumbed to fever and ague, vectored no doubt by the 'Scots Grey' mosquitoes that have always been a scourge in the St Lawrence region. Febrile and painfully hungry, the group bumped into a trio of white men in similar distress. These were Andrew Scott, Thomas Ross and William Fraser of the Hornet Bank property in the Dawson River country.

This last man was already a legend — someone to beware.

Three years previously, in 1857, infamy had come to Hornet Bank when eight of the Fraser family and three employees were killed in a dawn raid by a large party of Aborigines. With hindsight the attack can be understood as a reasoned reaction to an ugly brawl of land seizures and sexual predation that the Native Police had loosed upon the region during the foregoing months. Many colonists and Aborigines from all over Queensland claimed that a council of war had been convened that year by Aborigines at the Bunya feast, where the Native Police had been damned by speakers from several tribes. An eminent warrior called Bielbah was believed to have been commissioned at Bunyah to head up the black resistance. Bielbah's reputation had grown great among Queensland blacks since he had recently coordinated several raids on livestock and homesteads in the Dawson River country.

Contrary to the Bunya council's schemes, however, the raid on Hornet Bank failed to stem the white advance. In effect, it caused a surge of bloodletting all over the frontier. White reprisals raged into a blitz that shoved the frontier north and west suddenly in a convulsion of revenge. Fraser and his heavily armed allies took to the tribes with every weapon they could carry. As obsessive as Frederick Wheeler, but with a different sense of self-righteousness, Fraser was grief plus ire. Tales circulated throughout the colony of how he had refused to leave the scene of his misery, choosing instead to range the country in quest of land and retribution. Or rather, he was searching out land *as* retribution. Eventually he would turn his vengeance into a career by taking rank in the Native Police, but for now he was a bloodstained entrepreneur.

In their encounter with Mackay's feverish crew, Fraser and his offsiders conceded that they were behind the vanguard for the moment, so they tagged on to the larger party and ached their way back toward Rockhampton. Soon they all encountered dray tracks that led them to a new property being developed at Collaroy by Dan Connor, formerly of Marlborough Station. Connor invited everyone to camp, recuperate and divulge a little about where they'd been. This is the scene that tells more than Mackay knew. It offers an image that helps us re-read the journal not as a well-resolved narrative of colonial adventure and success but as an edgy report from a disturbed place and time.

---

brinkmen

Here they were, at the limits of the European land survey that was blotching out north from Rockhampton: a camp full of brinkmen, everyone restless for acquisition; archetypal venturers who could not rest within tame circuits of small-pasture husbandry. They were of that energetic class of horizon-broaching men who had brought a new, adversarial attitude to the country. As they swapped stories, they must have been eyeing one another charily, each man knowing that his companions here at the campfire were simultaneously allies and competitors. Here was the logic of the new world in microcosm: the settlers knew the aggression and competition in their hearts but they were masking it also by speaking out loud in terms of the civility and comradeship they needed to rally against all the surrounding brute nature that they wanted to grab. This was similar to the duplicity that had been enacted recently by the officers of the Native Police when they wrote their reports of 'dispersals' and 'disciplines' in the region. The settlers knew that the country had been subdued for them by the frontier guerrillas in the Native Police. Therefore the new world was not brave so much as it was riven by the contradiction of knowing-and-dissembling, of simultaneous realising and denying. These men were all saying things at the campfire, but they were refusing to admit or divulge much at all. With one breath they professed the brotherhood of their whiteness, with the next they worked for advantage in stratagems of their entrepreneurial rivalry.

In this campfire tableau we can see the moral of the John Mackay story: from the frontier days through the squatters' times and right up to the present day, most districts of Queensland have been defined by this paradoxically knowing silence, this habitual, politic taciturnity which has enabled men to know and concurrently to deny the violence and theft in their heritage. Around their campfire, these men were practising the wary sufferance of each other's presence.

Everyone on the frontier knew that legions of competitors were always trying to stake claims. And because the country itself was proving so intractable, no single faction managed to settle comprehensively enough to become the dominant or 'normal' force there. Each different group had its own presumptions and obsessions, its own story-systems for self-representation and self-justification. Which meant that each group kept itself distinct. Clusters of like-minded allies looked at all the others, seeing them as troublesome and unreliable. In the unwelcoming Capricornian environment, where even the weather never stopped threatening varieties of violence, settlement involved force, constant vigilance and irresolution. Thus the colony was cobbled out of discordances and unending adversity rather than formed conclusively by something as credible as a class of people who were happily persuaded by their own myths of colonial heroism and triumph. Rather, each of the several factions of Central Queensland learned to know itself by keeping cunning and silent in this geography and history which constantly produced more feelings of exile than belonging. The landscape took shape through a series of contingent grabs and reactions rather than according to a well-defined worldview served by a clearly narrated plan. No single, over-arching story defined the place.

---

detritus of others

Into the brigalow country, close behind the brinkmen, there soon came a retinue of secondary country-consumers and camp-followers who knew land in the same way they knew good fortune — chancily, hungrily and rarely for long. This was the start of the culture of short-stay itinerancy that has defined much of rural Queensland. Here were a squabble of people gleaning subsistence off others and off the detritus of others. They were gardeners, builders, grog-makers, whores and procurers, prospectors, mariners, shepherds and odd-job bodies-for-hire. They were the workforce on the grasslands, the mining sites and the fisheries which Noel Loos has identified as the three dominant 'frontiers of racial contact' in tropical Queensland. And they formed the first mass of capitalism in the country, tussling with one another and with the environment for the chance of some quickly wrested wealth.

deracination

So the colony north of Rockhampton was a splintered society comprised of caste upon caste of differentiated newcomers. Conciliation was not a motive here. Rather, conflict, coercion and dissimulation defined the 'community'. With the push for national unification gathering force in the south, there was little hope of spruiking a singular Australia to the motley agglomeration of people in the tropics, particularly when one considers that the idea of Federation was yet another intruding alien influence. And as for the metaphors that inform utopian multiculturalism nowadays — the 'symphony' of influences, the interweaving of strands into robust social fabrics — these wishful images simply did not apply here at the turn of the twentieth century. Rather, a society was forming from the deracination of human communities and from the exploitation rather than the integration and stewardship of land.

estranged mentalities

In 1863, when James Morrill turned up on the edge of the Port Denison settlement, he represented an opportunity and a threat for settlers all over the ever-expanding Australian colonies. Embodying an unpredictable meld of psychological and philosophical boundaries and definitions, he had come back with some skills in negotiating between estranged mentalities and cultures. He was the same as the Europeans, but he had also become something other. Could the settlers learn from him? Could Morrill survive the great shock of being wrapped again in whiteness? Was he some kind of prototype, a model of an unpredictable future Australian?

Time disallowed these questions. Morrill died soon after his 'repatriation', and the challenges he carried dropped from sight as citizens throughout Australia were deciding, usually more unconsciously than consciously, that whatever was not European was not to be acknowledged. This narrowing of minds, legislated via the xenophobic edicts of the new federal parliament, gripped the white society despite the fact that a great range of peoples had always formed the Australian populace. In tropical Queensland, where cultural differences were already pronounced on the polyglot cattle runs, mining fields and sugar paddocks, the white settlers recoiled from the complexity of a future that might involve so much continuous alteration and negotiability. Unable to invent comforting myths about consultation and constant mutation, yet sensing also that stories of manifest destiny and triumphs in the tropics were implausible, most Central Queensland communities learned to live in a mythologic vacuum, without justifying stories or founding myths. So the colonists took shelter in tight-lipped vigilance and became adept at ignoring troublesome traces in the past, present and future.

What does this silence communicate, ultimately? Confusion. Vulnerability. Fear and hatred also, as well as a kind of self-assertiveness, given that the decision to be quiet can be a deliberate choice. All these elementary emotions agitated in the Queensland settlements. Perhaps this is obvious, but a history of such feelings is rarely offered when one tries to imagine how the shape of the past has pushed into the present of colonial societies. And sure enough, there *are* stories that touch on these feelings, but they're never celebrated with the fervour of a good, persuasive myth. The stories that really illuminate the colonial past are almost always passing anecdotes and throwaway quips. Which is not to say they are unimportant.

'I do not think the rule applies'

For example, consider the following tale of quiet befuddlement in the memoirs of Edward Kennedy, an old colonist who spent his youth in the Queensland Native Police. In the tranquility of retirement, as he recollects the details of his boundary-riding life, a 'meaningless' event burrs away at Kennedy's account of the things and people he has encountered. He remembers a moment that he can neither expel nor accommodate neatly with a well-resolved moral:

> It has been said by some that *all* human beings when at the last, in extremis, lift up their eyes to heaven.
>
> This may be generally true, but from my own observation I do not think the rule applies to the Australian black ... Near Rockhampton a black fellow had committed a diabolical outrage on a white woman, from the effects of which she died. The man was sentenced to be hanged, and I was present at the execution. I remember that all the jailbirds were turned into the yard to witness the ceremony. Standing as I was, immediately in front of the gallows, I had ample opportunity of judging in what manner the murderer comported himself.
>
> Up to the very last moment he had use of his eyes, he scanned the forest, the valleys and waters, but never for one instant turned his eyes Heavenwards.

No matter how much Kennedy longs to put this recollection to rest, he fails to compose the homily that might have given him some complacency or moral supremacy. He can only report that the black man who chose to dedicate his last moments to the forests and waters could not be dragged into Christianity. Kennedy's writing falters for a moment here, his self-assertion suspended. Then he leaves the incident, trying to forget it even as he shows he cannot. By the time we turn the page, the memoirs are plodding unconvincingly again through their wishful apologies for white destiny, proceeding through avoidance, as if the philosophical disturbance of the black man could be ignored despite the force of the memory of him. Doubt disturbs the congratulation and celebration that the text is meant to encourage.

refusing

Australian Federation was supposed to be a galvanising climax to a myth of burgeoning security and wealth offered to a freshly integrated society. But in violently born enclaves like Central Queensland, too many people knew this kind of narrative to be a fiction which, no matter how much they desired it, could not be credited. Federation was a rite-of-passage which was supposed to construct a singular audience — the proud and confident nation. But in the tropics it actually addressed a dispersion of citizens jangled with scepticism and with too much tight-lipped, deliberate ignorance. Like the brinkmen around Dan Connor's campfire, too many Australian citizens faced the new century knowing what they were obliged to suppress if they wanted to maintain the illusion of national integrity amidst the cast of bad-faith actors who took benefit from Federation. Too many citizens knew the tight-lipped face they had to wear in this country they could never admit they had taken.

Over time, white settlers tried to become accustomed

to denying that otherness was in their midst even as they put it to work, dispatched it or imprisoned it. Great tracts of the landscape spurned agriculture and pastoral profitability, but the colonists continued trying to wring profits from it. Aboriginal people were everywhere and culturally distinct but the colonists avoided the quandary of them by insisting that they were dying out. This is how the colony was maintained: by sensing but trying not to see, by fearing and knowing but trying not to acknowledge.

Version 6

Ancestors Adrift

One morning in 1884, just outside Mackay, a ship full of labourers from the South Sea Islands was tarrying alongside the pilot boats. They were sheltering behind Flat Top Island, at the mouth of the Pioneer River, while the waters swirled unpredictably in the channels and sandbanks that formed the dangerous harbour. The weather had been big and green for several days, and everyone on board was sick with delay. This was not only because of the waves, for during several changes of tide, the pilots had been stalling and debating whether to allow this ship safe passage into the town.

Everyone was nervous, on sea and land. Ashore, councillors were loath to authorise the mooring because of rumours that confusion and unrest were brewing on board. The townsfolk had heard that the cargo was New Irelanders and that these first-time recruits were the wildest cannibals ever brought to civilisation. Down south in Brisbane, parliament was being briefed about the standoff, for they were worried that accusations of slave trading could rise up again if it transpired that these 'recruits' had not been thoroughly informed about what they were shipping off to do in Queensland. Talk was spreading down the eastern seaboard that the New Irelanders had been kidnapped rather than recruited.

When the ship was finally given clearance to dock, there was a great hubbub on the wharf. Two of the New Irelanders jumped into the tumult, disappearing amidst a throng of Melanesian labourers who had come in from the farms. White policemen waded straightaway through the crowd, but the ship-jumpers had vanished.

Gossip jittered around the region. The runaways had been seen here; animals had been killed there. Back at the docks, white men with rifles refused to let the remaining Islanders disembark. Nervous days went by.

Out in the countryside, a posse rode into Sarina where they had heard that a Chinaman and a white woman camping beside Plane Creek had lost their little boy. Searchers could find no trace of the lad, other than his hat, which was lying near the remnants of a recent campfire. A gang of vigilantes flattened the bush along the creek-banks where Aborigines still gathered for hunting and shelter.

The yelling men trapped the two New Irelanders within a shout of the campfire where the hat had been found. With no proof at all, word went round that the Melanesians had eaten the child. A lynching seemed likely. The runaways were trussed up and trucked back into town on a dray, but in the meantime some of the plantation managers had calmed the waiting mob by reminding everyone how do-gooders in Brisbane were looking for any excuse to phase out the labour schemes. How much would the Southerners love it, the managers asked, to hear of mob-rule in the tropics?

So the white people governed their fractiousness and hoisted the runaways back on the ship. The entire contingent of Islanders and recruiters was escorted out of the harbour and told to sail north.

---

the material world of their exile

During four decades from the mid-1860s onwards, more than 60,000 Melanesian labourers, predominantly from the Solomon Islands and Vanuatu, spent three-year terms toiling the dangerous chores of the Queensland sugar industry. As years went by, approximately 25 per cent of the recruits signed up for a second term, and at the height of the labour trade, in the early 1880s, there were more than 13,000 Islanders living in the cane country of Queensland. The 1888 workforce of the Ashburton Mill, on the outskirts of Mackay, was typical: forty-seven Europeans filled managerial and skilled-labour positions above a staff of three

Chinese, five Javanese and two hundred and twenty Melanesians. The Islanders were regarded as the Europeans' insurance against the disease, exhaustion and moral decadence that were thought to be endemic to all tropical exertion.

During the 1860s when the labour trade was in its early stages, deception and kidnapping (known colloquially as 'blackbirding') were commonplace whenever recruiting ships came to the Islands. But by the time one generation of Melanesians had seen the traders continue to collect and return most of the young men, it seems that all parties roughly agreed on conditions of payment, accommodation and repatriation. Indeed, by the mid-1880s, recruiters and plantation managers were complaining that the Solomon Islands and Vanuatu people knew the conditions so well that they were becoming too canny in their bargaining, not allowing enough profit to be wrung from their persons. Several field-managers were curious to know whether some newer, less savvy recruits could be exploited. Hence the arrival of boatloads from New Ireland and New Britain, where the contractual conditions had not yet become well-agreed, and where maverick recruiters might snare some boatloads before the government-authorised labour-agents could establish offices, protocols and go-betweens.

As the panic around the New Ireland ship-jumpers indicated, the potential for confusion was extreme when unaccustomed recruits arrived in Mackay. The two runaways must have decided they could not survive in the world of the sugar farmers, but how did they fare in the alien bush? What horticultural knowledge informed their foraging in the mosquito-clouded scrub? During their days in the wild, did they encounter other Islanders who were working the canefields nearby? (Melanesian cane-cutters in Queensland were renowned for walking great distances through the bush, either to visit friends or to visit vengeance upon enemies in outlying plantations.) If such meetings occurred, was there any fellow-feeling, or were these black people as alien to each other as white men were to all Melanesians? Did the New Irelanders see any of the battles between Santo Islander and Malaitan canecutters, battles that are still celebrated in the oral histories of Mackay? Did they communicate, to any halting degree, with the Aborigines and the Chinese who were grubbing livelihoods along the creek bank? Did they see anything of the Sunday hunting-parties (said to have been tacitly sanctioned by the canefield managers) involving Malaitans in pursuit of Aborigines? What unknown beasts, native or feral, did the New Irelanders devour to keep themselves alive? Did they try their own traditional fishing techniques to snare food from the creek? Did they risk eating the offal that floated down from the campsites and slaughter-yards further upstream?

These are all questions about everyday life and the meanings that people don't even pause to consider when they feel 'settled' in a landscape. During the

1880s, however, in the environs of Mackay, none of these simplicities could be taken for granted. In the Capricorn tropics, many radically different cultures endured spiritual dearth in the material world of their exile. For example, Chinese migrants worked mineral leases and garden plots in a world out of time. They stayed in the district just long enough to grab quick profit and then returned to a homeland where village traditions and ancestral obligations helped them find their bearings again. As for the local Aborigines, they were now living in a broken system, their land and rivers partitioned and churned up in new patterns of pasture and profiteering that disregarded how the country had always been tended before the Native Police had come in.

Into this context of alteration and exploitation, thousands of Islander canecutters were unloaded. They must have wondered how to live carefully in this range country that was so unlike the mountainous islands of home. Obviously this place must have been policed by *somebody's* ancestor-spirits, but how to heed them when the environment seemed so inscrutable, so devoid of Melanesian stories? As events would unfold, this new ground would soon be tempered with large numbers of Islander spirits, but it would have been cold comfort for the labourers to foresee how this would transpire.

identities all atomise

If all the immigrant factions in Central Queensland shared one thing in their mutual estrangement, it was a sense of how disorganised and disintegrated life had become in this place where so many different peoples had to make history out of alienation and temporary accommodations. Nowadays we look back and call this tangle of struggles 'colonialism' (wishing to believe it past). And we use particular names to identify the players in this drama, names like 'Melanesian', 'Kanaka', 'settler'. But as soon as they are named, these identities all atomise once we begin to understand them better.

For example, the 'Melanesians' who worked the cane-fields were often treated as one group, but they were of astonishing (and often incommensurable) variety. There were New Irelanders, Vanuatuans, New Britainers and Solomon Islanders, all inhabiting different systems of history and belief. Even within the category of the 'Solomon Islands', let's say, there were hundreds of communities from that starburst of islands. A 'Solomon Islander' from Malaita may have been a foreigner to a 'Solomon Islander' from Guadalcanal. Also, people from any single island were differentiated by gender, by their vocations (fisher, gardener, canoe-maker) and by languages, depending on whether they hailed from the beaches or from the inland bush-villages.

Furthermore, by the time the labour-recruiting ships

had started working the south seas, Christian missionaries had already been in the islands for at least a generation, particularly in the beach communities near the copra plantations where Christianity and mercantilism had already intertwined. Indeed, many of the recruiting vessels were owned by Godeffroy und Sohn, a German copra-harvesting company which also financed dozens of collecting forays carried out by vagabond agents who gathered Pacific artefacts for museums which were drawing huge paying crowds in cities such as Hamburg. So, a significant proportion of Pacific people had begun to negotiate several theological and mercantile systems and they were accustomed to white men by the time the canefield agents began anchoring off their beaches. No one was leading a simple or carefree island life.

More than half the labourers who came to the Mackay environs hailed from villages with missionary schools. In fact, some recruits would have enlisted to escape the Christian regimes that they felt were poisoning their villages. But it seemed there was no avoiding the crucified god — the Islanders soon discovered that the canefields were under his sway too. From 1882 onward, for example, Mrs Mary Goodwin ran a Christian school and chapel for Melanesians in Mackay. This was a private venture, but it wasn't long before the Anglican church also established missions alongside plantations, from Rockhampton all the way up the coast. Fresh converts were wooed in Queensland at the same time as the church preached to those Islanders who were already in the faith. Thus the canefields around Mackay were spirited by a melange of 'theologies' commingling Melanesian ancestor-worship and several Christian catechisms.

Even so, despite the preponderance of evangelism in the Pacific, the labour trade in Queensland did not become less 'heathen' over time. In later years of recruiting, as the coastal communities drove harder bargains, most agents began negotiating with workers from outlying islands and from bush and mountain villages away from the churches and copra groves of the beaches. In these more isolated communities, contact with missionaries and European traders had been limited and the indigenous rituals governed by the magic-makers and the ancestors were still powerful. These newer recruits brought relatively 'undiluted' Islander cultures into the canefields. Moreover there was another category of labourers: the Islanders who insisted that their time in Queensland was a purely secular interlude spent in a temporary vacuum of spirit.

The Queensland Melanesian communities did not become progressively more assimilated to European ways. For all the growing agitation for homogeneity in a White Australia, Central Queensland was not tending that way. Later in the history of the labour trade, for example, any shipload en route to tropical Queensland might have been classifiable like this:

25% 'returning workers' who had already spent a three-year stint in the canefields and were seeking extra finance for particular trade items that they had set their minds to; 25% young people who were seeking status through both the acquisition of goods and the stories associated with worldly experience; 20% who could blame their plight on European traders' lies and artifice; 15% who were 'rented out' by their relatives or their communities; 10% who were fleeing enmity at home; and possibly 5% who were escaping famine caused by cyclone or drought.

Defined under the one name of 'Kanaka', a name used by the Europeans to place their labourers on a scale of worth just above the lowly designation of 'Aborigine', an astonishingly relativistic and politically astute populace constructed their migrant lives.

It is not clear how many of the Europeans involved in the labour trade knew of the complexities in the workforce that they were naming and marshalling. Consider the nuances of the word 'Kanaka', for instance. It came from no Melanesian language. It was originally a Polynesian term for 'person' or 'man' and it probably came into the English language because European whalers and merchant mariners had been trading words and grammatical patterns with Polynesian crew members since the 1770s. (Also, the punning similarity between 'Kanaka' and 'cane-hacker' appealed to plantation wags.) In more recent times, the word has been commandeered by Melanesian people as part of a political strategy to seize control of discourses that colonists once used to define and demean indigenous cultures. (Of course the word 'Melanesian' itself is tangled in this history.)

The classification 'Kanaka' was based on a misrecognition, therefore — many different entities were all homogenised under one label. Such confusions of definition proliferated in Central Queensland. This 'entanglement' is one way to understand colonialism: it is a contest of interpretive categories and techniques colliding in a destabilised world where meanings, values and powers of self-determination all agitate against one another. In the canefields, the plantation owners classified the black labourers as units of work and profit. When the boats came in to the Queensland ports and gangs of Islanders were assigned to the plantations, the white foremen often assembled the recruits according to physical size, regardless of which places they came from. As a result, cane-cutting teams could be comprised of many language groups and family and village allegiances, all of which may have been unsympathetic or perhaps even antipathetic to one another. But the plantation administrators preferred not to acknowledge the 'native' distinctions between, say, Vanuatuans and Solomon Islanders.

The colonial logic of profit thus ignored the logics of indigenous cultures. Most field managers insisted on talking to all the Melanesians in the *lingua franca* of 'bichelemar', the 'melange of Melanesian grammar and English-derived labels', which spread across the Southwest Pacific and eventually became Kanaka Pidgin

English. At the same time as they became adept at pidgin, however, the Melanesian workers also maintained their own dialects. Within a labour regime that treated them as objects, comrades spoke to each other like autonomous subjects, in the specific languages of home, in languages which excluded and mystified the Europeans. This was one way the Islanders showed that they were not passive nor even particularly comprehensible to the colonists, and it was one way the Europeans might have begun to understand that there was more happening in the tropics than could be contained in colonial assumptions.

spiritual credit

Amidst the *mercantile* exchanges, there also must have been some significant transactions in Melanesian *metaphysics*. Notions such as 'credit', 'trade' and 'debt', which the Europeans invoked habitually, were also special concerns for the Islander recruits. For the Islanders, though, these notions were more spiritual than commercial. The traditional tokens of Islander 'trade' — pigs, shells, yams, fish — came directly from the land and the sea, which is to say wealth and indebtedness came from nature and were therefore related to transcendent forces. Even when Islanders began to covet guns and clocks and hats, it seems most of them never forgot that the materials of the world came and went with the whims of the ancestral spirits, who colluded with fatality at every moment and in every object. The canecutters' traditional customs assured them they toiled in a world ruled by magic and metaphysical obligation.

Clive Moore has written some of the most perceptive accounts of Melanesian experience in Queensland. He insists on explaining the Islanders' economies in immaterial terms:

> Major exchanges of commodities took place between individuals and whole kin groups: foods, building materials, ceremonial payments like brideprice, murder rewards and the products used in mortuary feasts. Group payments could be made for individual needs, but reciprocity bound the receiver to the giver. All these exchanges allowed metaphysical communication, linking living people to their ancestors, the ultimate source of *mamana*.

Mamana is a kind of spiritual credit whereby people are graded and obligated in the social and cosmic order. To believe in *mamana* is to believe that any transaction in the material realm also involves moral power; one negotiates not only with objects and other human beings but also in the presence of all the spirit energies and ancestors who have been entangled before you. The ancestors are not confined to some redundant past.

In a world suffused with *mamana* it was (and is) no matter of idle curiosity to contemplate trading yourself to work in faraway places, across ocean 'roads' not traditionally protected by the credit systems of your ancestors and your village community. Moreover, during the late nineteenth century, Islander migration was overwhelmingly a male activity, which meant that a labourer's life had to be improvised without many of the gender-defined directives and responsibilities — woman to man, man to woman, woman to earth and sea, man to earth and sea — that had always secured traditional societies.

How intricately nuanced every action and event must have been for most of the Queensland canecutters! How much disquiet was endured in the canefields, how much perplexity in the absence of everyday spiritual guidelines. How disturbing and discordant each canecutter's three years of exile must have seemed, away from the ancestrally tuned homeland, surrounded as these canecutters were by omens and opportunities that were not customary. As all the different Islanders gathered in the Queensland canefields, quick deals were struck chancily with great cosmic powers even as everyone persevered with the intriguing business of adapting, coping and sometimes profiting. In quest of adventure and gain, the canecutters knew that they risked trading with forces of death whenever they negotiated with the labour agents. Thus the Islanders imported a complex system of spiritual liability into country which had already been bent metaphysically awry by the frontier violence that had assailed the Aboriginal spirit-world. A colony always gets built in the spirit world at the same time as claims get staked in the geographical world.

---

darkened European minds

At the time of the Islander trade in Queensland, evolutionary theory with its dismissive presumptions about 'savagery' had recently darkened European minds against the wit in indigenous mentalities. Kanaka sophistication was unthinkable to most plantation managers. Melanesian people, on the other hand, were well-prepared to understand the theories and practices of colonialism. Islander communities had passed on tales of white-skinned profiteers ever since 1606 when Pedro Fernandes de Quiros had stopped several days at the island he named Espiritu Santo. The stories about de Quiros had currency particularly in the Vanuatu group, but they may well have been transmitted along many of the trade routes around the Southwest Pacific. Earlier memories of Mendana in the Solomons probably circulated too. Later tales of sandalwooders and whalers were incorporated into Islanders' lore during the early decades of the nineteenth century. On top of all this Islander savviness, the mercantilism of the copra plantations and the missionaries' complicity in the cargo systems was thoroughly understood by the time the Queensland labour-traders began to call.

---

good custom

Most Melanesian societies are adept at travel and they understand how itinerancy requires adaptation and the ability to negotiate with other mentalities. Traditionally, Islanders were trained to be relativistic and to recognise (though not necessarily to admire) the existence of other cultures and the validity of multiple levels of reality. Flexibility and pragmatism were built into every-day life as Islanders learned to live in ever-shifting environments. In one system of metaphors that is wide-spread across the Pacific, many Islanders define themselves by valorising the *stability* of the land that stands firm in the sea at the same time as they celebrate the *mobility* of the canoe that enables the daily fishing excursions and the ritual 'custom journeys' which ma-turing young people often make beyond their local environments. On many islands this doubleness of ex-istence is understood by imagining every person as a tree which is simultaneously always the canoe that can be fashioned from it. Each holds the matter and spirit of the other, the tree and the canoe. On the island of Tanna in Vanuatu, for example, the tree of your person keeps you strong and reliable because of its roots in the earth while the canoe helps you know yourself as part of a dynamic fleet which is always exploring and responding to the shifting patterns of oceanic existence.

In many Pacific pidgin languages the canoe voyage is translated as 'go walkabout'. It is usually deemed 'good custom'. In traditional times, one might have justifiably travelled away from the village for maturation rituals, lineage business, convivial visiting, ceremonial feasting or to escape some dispute or potential humiliation. Sometimes the custom journey would be done alone, sometimes with companions. In most cases, travellers expected to return repeatedly to the place of their birth, to their tree-ground. When colonialism intervened, traditional voyaging became intertwined with the modern Western ideas of migration and exile. Thousands of Islanders began to experiment with these new systems, undertaking labour-journeys and working their way back successfully and profitably, acting cannily amidst the upheaval, incorporating the experience in time-honoured practices of personal and communal definition.

Cruel and duplicitous as the labour trade often was, it was not something simply 'done to' a victimised Pacific people. Within the endlessly ponderable complexities of colonialism, the labour trade was also wilfully 'enacted' by a variety of Melanesian societies. Once the Islanders realised that outside forces were bringing great changes into the ocean world, they engaged with this new incursive reality. By the time the Queensland labour trade had been established just a few years, detailed analytical knowledge of it was already circulating through a vast span of islands. Recruits knew the names and reputations of cruel foremen at particular plantations; returning labourers told of pleasures to be found in the red-lanterned 'Yokahama Lane' which led down to Mackay's Chinatown; old campaigners offered advice about which trade goods were most easily procured in which towns up and down the Queensland coast; all over the Southwest Pacific, fabulous accounts were given of the Mackay racecourse and its rituals of gambling. People from a wide arc of islands learned to recognise which recruiting boats ought to be avoided and which ones offered conditions they were prepared to take a chance on. Melanesians assessed all the circulating information and evaluated the options available for migration and experimentation. Once the trade had been established for a few years in any particular area, kidnapping by recruiters seems to have declined. Seeing the relentlessness of European incursion, Islanders began to investigate it and engage with it. And they soon learned about other indentured labour regimes — the nickel mines of New Caledonia, the mixed plantations of Fiji and Samoa, the huge industrial-scale groves of coconut in Vanuatu. Generally speaking, the trade goods and conditions in Queensland were considered at least as profitable as anywhere else on offer in the new world of labour-voyaging.

Of course, voyaging always entailed risk. The great

challenge of travel was not only that it might lead an individual to wisdom, esteem and material wealth, nor even that it was simply dangerous in a physical sense; voyaging could also cause deep ructions in the metaphysical world that Islanders were obliged to tend with their daily ceremonies and exertions. The greatest danger was that labour-migrants might find themselves psychologically and morally adrift if they left their 'tree-ground', never to find the fellowship and security of their proper 'canoe-community' in the new territories. They ran the risk of losing *mamana* and ceasing to exist. Without strong, 'lateral' structures of communication and group support, Islanders could plunge into chaos once they were detached from the place and people of their birth. As a Malaitan proverb advises, when a tree loses its branches and is wrenched from the ground, it 'rolls downhill and cannot be stopped'. This, in part, explains why large groups of villagers usually recruited together and struggled to stay in communication with one another during the three-year terms of Queensland work. On Sundays, when Queensland government policy decreed that no field-work was allowed, hundreds of Melanesians used to walk huge distances through the bush to visit canoe-comrades. Thus, even within the individualistic cultures of the European world, versions of traditional, 'communal' ethics guided many of the canecutters.

The notion of canoe-loyalty also explains why only 6.5 per cent of Melanesian recruits in Queensland were women. Traditional migration systems usually allowed 'dispensable' young men to leave home. Generally speaking, men were not expected to heed fatherly responsibilities until their mid-twenties, whereas women were meant to be bearing children by the time they were in their late teens. Thus collective lore endorsed the wandering of young men but was more cautious about the 'release' of young women. The women who did leave must be counted extraordinarily courageous or under extreme duress. Some may have seized opportunities for escaping onerous bride contracts or for satisfying 'errant' needs or curiosities. In many cases women were kidnapped by the recruiters, for carnal purposes, but there are also accounts of women hailing launches from deserted stretches of beach where they had momentarily escaped the scrutiny of village law. Also, there is no good reason to assume that Islander-women did not also hanker after the material wealth, influence and adventure that enticed many of the male recruits.

Perhaps the voyaging is better understood as purposeful, political research. While powerful new worlds were pressing in on the islands, Pacific people began to analyse the changes, to see how the traditional life of canoe-and-tree, of roads and rituals involving circular migration, could absorb the new experiences. From the Islanders' perspective, voyaging to research the incursive culture was a necessary business. For the Islanders themselves, the trade seems to have threaded itself into customary practices and worked an effective dialectic between coercion and allure.

---

the wishful habit of denial

With all this research and resistance being enacted by indigenous peoples, the Central Queensland canefields were much more than the theatre of social Darwinism that many whites expected. The Islanders brought several active systems of belief with them and while the indigenous cosmologies were challenged and radically adapted in contact with European realities, no single common sense ruled on this contentious colonial ground. By the time the indentured labourers began to arrive in great numbers, Frederick Wheeler and his colleagues in the Native Police had already mauled and dispersed the indigenous consciousness (as well as many settler-mentalities) in Central Queensland. As the Capricorn frontier was transformed into an austere and attenuated stretch of settlement with sugar plantations and cattle stations at either end, the bloody heritage of the Aboriginal land wars kept niggling at many settlers' memories. Thus Central Queensland became suffused with the fears as well as the desires of a huge array of people recently jumbled together there, at odds with one another.

From the 1860s, in the pages of Capricornian newspapers, disappearances, ugly domestic demise and barely comprehended diseases were reported almost obsessively. This was a young society in splints of anxiety and growing into distress. A society with metaphysical turbulence in its foundations.

But even as the colony was steeped in so much recent quandary, the wishful habit of denial continued to define the culture, cloaking a thorough knowledge of how the society had been inaugurated through violence and land theft. And now, added to the heritage of the land wars, there was this labour trade which nobody dared analyse too closely in case it really appeared to be some kind of slavery or ethnic obliteration. Thus the communities that were grafting around the Capricorn badlands became evermore dependent on a kind of procedural ignorance, and thus became evermore suspicious, uncertain and anxious. The more habitual the practice of denial, the more edgy the communities became as the white people simultaneously knew and refused to know the violence behind their everyday lives.

death was everywhere

At some level of consciousness, a few settlers dreaded the spiritual obligations that the colony was accruing and ignoring. Perhaps this kind of apprehensiveness had spurred Robert McGavin to sue for the punishment of Frederick Wheeler at Banchory Station. In jittery enclaves that were getting established along the coast north of Rockhampton, some settlers were struggling with a barely grasped sense of apprehension, a dreadful premonition that one's life might be violently ambushed at any moment by some force larger than secular. By the time the Melanesian cultures had entered the colony, therefore, death seemed to be extending its claims on the landscape.

For one thing, disease had a carnival amongst the Melanesian labour recruits. Measles, flu and dietary shock claimed stunning numbers in the canecutters' camps. In 1875 an epidemic of measles killed three hundred and seventy-eight Islanders in Maryborough alone. A decade later, in Mackay, where dysentery claimed twenty-five workers each year, a strain of influenza which was benign in the European community culled more than eight hundred Islanders from a population of approximately four thousand. This was 1884, the same year the ship-jumping New Irelanders had hidden in the Plane Creek scrub, which partially explains why the town had been in such an incendiary mood.

For the canecutters, the 1884 flu was brusque and hateful somehow. Islanders would wake coughing. By mid-morning they were itching with a red rash all over their chests. Soon after, they were wheezing in the shade, heads aching, bowels in spasm. By sunset they were dead in the fields. That year, the official mortality rate in the European population of Queensland was 1.6 per cent; amongst the labour-recruits it was underestimated by plantation accountants but still tallied a terrifying 15.8 per cent.

So Death was a daily presence in the lives of the canecutters. And when bodies fell, plantation management rarely accorded them ceremonial dispatch with prayers or Islander ceremonies. The Europeans usually buried black corpses in unmarked graves, no special effort accorded to death certificates or autopsies. In the Melanesian communities this carelessness must have caused great unease. The disquiet can be heard, one hundred years on, in the testimony of Noel Fatnowna, a canecutter descendant who was an ambulance driver in Mackay during the 1970s:

> Some of the old Kanaka men worked here for fifty years. When they died, they were carried away. Even in death they didn't even want us. They took us to a part of the cemetery they called the 'heathen ground'. In that 'heathen ground' they buried Chinese, Japanese, Malays, Indonesians and Islanders. Today when I drive around the district I know the exact places where our people lie buried. My father was a lay preacher and buried many people. Many people. Unmarked graves in canefields, some with roads going over them.

Disease took a grievous toll in the region. But sickness was not the only reaper. Melanesian communities traditionally revere mortality and constantly seek to be engaged in the way death tempers the forces of life. To honour death, to manage its power through ceremony seems to have been a basic tenet in all Islander societies, and there is little doubt that a 'moral economy' of mortality was imported into Queensland from some of the islands.

Many Melanesian societies practised a culture of life-taking — not the beastliness that the Europeans chose to perceive, but a lore-governed, occasional 'prioritising' of death in the metaphysical rhythms of the world. A system of revenge-murder had long been part of most island customs. But 'murder' is not a precise enough term in this context. The killings were more like an extreme attentiveness to the workings of the cosmos. In most Islander mentalities, death does not mark the end of an individual's life so much as it is part of a universal pattern ensuring that the society of the living is always garnering its energies and responsibilities through associations with the spirit world where the ancestors go. In a truly vital sense, people have their dead with them in all places at all times. Life would be incomplete and untenable otherwise.

ghosts and haunting

The landscape of the Islanders' exile was soon haunted by thousands of restless ancestors. It is no fanciful idiom to speak like this. To declare a place haunted is to understand how metaphysical debts work through the social histories of colonial landscapes to produce the delayed outbursting forces which killed Noel and Sophie Weckert and which maintain particular districts as badlands. In the Pacific Islands the 'spiritual economies' of ceremonial killing were understood and practised according to strict rules, but in Queensland the blood-accounting became much less manageable and comprehensible. Once the Islanders arrived in the Queensland canefields, they tried to ensure that their communal and metaphysical worlds were kept in some kind of harmony despite the mortality and normlessness that closed around them. Amidst all the diseases, the industrial accidents and the unpredictable vengeance-killings, Melanesian Death reached out frequently past the confinement of the Kanakas' camps to mark the rest of the Capricorn hinterland in ways that baffled the white settlers. European chroniclers in the sugar districts did not understand that there were 'legal' and spiritual dimensions to Melanesian 'violence', nor did they know that white people were sometimes incorporated into Islanders' mortal rituals. Colonists confirmed their own sense of civilised ascendancy by condemning a savage bloodlust and so they failed to recognise how Melanesian cultures regarded the ministering of death as a necessary part of responsible behaviour in a well-tended cosmos.

When Islanders imported their rites into Central

Queensland, they encountered European-induced Death already plundering black people unceremoniously. Disproportionate mortality had become historically normal in Central Queensland. And now Melanesian systems of revenge and ritual deposition were being ushered into the canefields too, thus reinforcing Death as a defining force in the landscape. If the Aborigines, the Chinese and the Islanders could have shared a language, they might all have remarked on the glut of unrested (and therefore troubled and troublesome) ancestors that were being produced in the colonial landscape. It was as if the *surface* of the land was all that the Europeans cared about. They seemed to have no concern for the deeper forces or spirits that created the country and maintained it in all its changeable depths and charges.

blood bounty

In a sample of four hundred and twenty Islanders' deaths documented in Mackay, Clive Moore found records of nineteen 'suicides' and thirty-two homicides. Taking into account the non-reporting of many more disappearances and 'accidental' demises which could be added to a murder-tally, it is evident that something 'methodical' was occurring with violent death in the canefields. As Moore remarks, 'the incidents seen and reported by Europeans were only a small part of the total number', and although 'the sugar-fields were a non-traditional situation, the Queensland setting may have provoked an even greater degree of violence than was normal in the islands'. This tallies with Melanesian storytellers' repeated claims that armed combat was a common afterhours activity among the canefield workers. At night-time, unknown to white overseers, huge fights were often staged between rival island groups from various plantations in the Mackay environs. Almost certainly, these hunts and battles were not simply 'recreational'. They were conducted under rules of honour and payback that had been laid down for centuries in the home islands. On Malaita, for example, combat was most often prompted by the violation of strict codes of sexual conduct, but thefts, curses or insults might also demand a violent response. If this led to the death of a member of your group, then you were entitled to take direct vengeance or to raise a blood bounty of pigs and other valuables, whereby you could then employ a *ramo* (mercenary warrior) to discipline the wrongdoer. Alternatively, a close relative or an agreed substitute victim could be chosen to settle the account. The *ramo* could fulfil his contracts by 'dramatic' confrontation, individual ambush or massive battalion-warfare (supported by a squad of warriors whom he paid with a percentage of the blood-bounty). The system of managed bloodshed almost certainly spread to Queensland where white colonists never seemed to consider that what the Islanders were engaged in was a rule-governed attempt to maintain a moral balance in the world of their exile.

When colonialism came into the Pacific, guns and machetes came too. They were the most coveted spoils of a Queensland labour term and they caused massive, convulsive imbalances in the 'exchange rates' of traditional mortal payback in the islands. By the end of a stint of work in Mackay, at least 70 per cent of recruits had purchased some kind of firearm. They could take the weapon back home and tote it as if they were ready, unceremoniously and unauthorised, to be ministers of death. All moral registers skewed as a result. Boastful displays of trade booty were almost mandatory, and if accidents occurred during the inevitable gunplay, new debts were often set up in addition to any vestigial offences. This almost invariably brought new *ramos* and would-be enforcers into the system, as newly aggrieved relatives put up fresh vengeance-money. In traditional times, the vengeance-blood could seep from one generation to the next. In the more disorderly world made by colonialism, the island communities must have haemorrhaged continuously.

The labour trade introduced peculiar sub-clauses into blood-law. For example, if a recruit failed to return home, presumed dead, and if no proxy came back with respectful reports plus the promised three-year salary, then villagers often felt entitled to demand payback from the European agent who had signed up the worker in the first place. Most recruiting agents had no idea that this obligation existed, and many never revisited an island after an initial tour of enlistment. Within Melanesian revenge-protocol, such a non-appearance could lead to substitute-payments being claimed, and the recompense could spread as far as Queensland. Clive Moore elaborates:

> Killing a European was acceptable compensation. The European did not need to be connected in any way with the Malaitan death, which probably explains a number of attacks against Europeans at Malaita and in Queensland, viewed by Europeans as totally unprovoked and irrational.

reading plots

Europeans' confusion about 'savagery' and their unwitting involvement in Melanesian blood-debts must have been compounded by the occasional 'unprovoked' attacks by Aborigines. Coincidentally, around Rockhampton from the 1860s onwards, the tribespeople had begun to enact a revenge-logic comparable to that of the Malaitans. In the context of the land wars, as Henry Reynolds has suggested, it is highly likely the Aborigines had a system of payback whereby a proxy life could be taken as recompense for an offence performed by a white person.

If the Europeans paid any attention to the rituals of the Melanesians and the Aborigines, it was usually only to condemn superstition and depravity. However, the settlers might have profited from learning how to 'read' the garden plots which many Vanuatuan canecutters cultivated on the edge of their barrack-yards around Mackay. Melanesian gardens are richly symbolic places where supplications, penance, trysts and treacheries are all possible. In any particular plot, an experienced garden-interpreter can recognise the recent fortunes and mood of an entire village. Traditionally, Melanesian gardens are not only provisioning grounds; they are also metaphysical marketplaces where blood-prices of food and 'shell-money' might get planted as signs that Death is required to settle some ruction. In the days when blood-money circulated customarily, the villagers and the *ramo* could visit the garden and 'read' what the custodians of the plot wished to be done and what they were prepared to pay. Thus grievance, justice and regeneration might take root and be nurtured to fruition in these 'cultured' enclaves in the 'wild' jungle. In a well-tended garden, the spirit and the matter of the world might burgeon so long as life and death were both honoured and nourished there.

It has been difficult to retrieve clear information about Melanesian gardening practices around the Capricorn hinterland. No-one can claim for certain that murder bounties were placed in Queensland plots. However, Clive Moore has found occasional newspaper comments about a particular 'class of boy' who inspired 'terrorism' and caused hardened colonists to 'sleep with a revolver near to hand'. As Moore suggests, these enigmatic characters are a little more comprehensible in the context of blood-money activities. Furthermore, Moore's research in oral testimonies from canecutter descendants, both in Mackay and in the islands, indicates that Malaitans prepared seriously for canefield combat and 'made up for any lack of fighting finesse by their sheer ferocity, achieved … by calling their *akalo* (ancestors) to aid them'. Also, the Tanna men from Vanuatu, with whom Malaitan canecutters often fought, were 'prone to using sorcery'. In each case, the empowering presence of ancestors and spirit-forces would have been confidently summoned only if the gardens that balanced life-and-death had been respectfully and successfully maintained. Almost certainly, nobody would have risked rousing the potentially wrathful spirits unless appropriate rituals and responsibilities were being observed.

counsel with a canefield sorcerer

On the evidence of several oral histories and family testimonies, it seems that practical magic was used every day in the Queensland plantations. In his memoirs, Noel Fatnowna recalls that as late the 1930s, 'the

Guadalcanal men were practising sorcery — worshipping the *akalo*'. Also, a small community of Vanuatuans were known to be still setting spells. 'The old men there would come out and do away with people who were going to marry into the New Hebridean race. Strange things used to happen. Men would die suddenly and nobody seemed to know what had happened.' From the 1860s onwards, secret burley herbs were grown in gardens, to be used as fishing spells by canecutters who went angling to supplement the unappealing plantation food. Also, love-magic was practised enthusiastically, with young men frequently seeking counsel with a canefield sorcerer to heighten their sexual attractiveness to the few Melanesian women who were working on the plantations. In Mackay, nearly every male canecutter would have had sufficient knowledge and permission to practise some magic for his own benefit.

Labourers were as attentive as possible to Island protocols. There are many aspects of canefield life that may have been somewhat ceremonial. For example, it may be pure coincidence that the women's work in the canefields consisted predominantly in mattocking weeds before the cane stalks grew tall, but it is possible that this was considered 'gardening' work and was therefore treated as a task appropriate to all the available women. For in most of the islands it was considered culturally inadvisable for men to be involved in any plant-raising chore unless it had some specifically designated magical associations. In Vanuatu, for example, the cultivation of yams was stringently governed by the sexual division of labour, but the growing of taro was a more informal exercise. There were many 'subdivisions' of 'regulations' about right behaviour relating to the growing of various staples. Most likely, the giant agricultural sugarcane would have been deemed a 'secular' or 'European' plant, even though a type of wild sugar-grass grew on many islands, and given that the gender sanctions governing cultivation were subtly different from island to island, there must have been some uncertainty about what the fields of young Queensland cane represented on a scale from the sacred to the profane. Should an Islander have been concerned about gardening 'protocols' in the sprouting canefields? This is just one more of the countless quandaries which must have worried the Melanesian labourers every day. In any event, one thing was clear: *cutting down* the cane in an industrial context was nothing like gardening and therefore such work threatened no gendered demarcations of sacred activity. So the Islander men felt authorised to go into the ripe fields with machetes.

The herbs, the gardens, the *akalo* and the magic cannot take effect without each other. It seems inconceivable that magic was not conjured by some of the canecutters. At the very least, given that so many of the men were prepared to go out fighting afterhours, they must have practised provisional (and perhaps 'experimental' or 'adaptive') ancestor-worship. Otherwise, no kind of metaphysical potency could have been anticipated in combat, which was an activity *never* to be undertaken frivolously.

With magic abounding in Melanesian mentalities, many of the deaths attributed to influenza in Queensland would have been understood as sorcery misadventures, or at least as the repercussions of some spiritual imbalance in their rapidly altering world. Modern ideas of antibodies and immunity notwithstanding, sorcery-fear is one factor explaining how little resistance the influenza sufferers seemed able to mount and how quickly they died. In the Queensland canefields, where the rules were so unfounded, worry about sorcery and spiritual debt must have been acute. In this place where the great ancestral patterns of the home village were not guaranteed, how much uncertainty must people have felt about the remedial ceremonies with which they were traditionally obliged to respond to sickness in the home village? Alternatively, if they had already transferred their allegiance to the God of the Christians, what doubts would have afflicted the canecutters as they lay sickly and uncertainly awaiting Christ's mercy? Could the crucified God prevail over the *akalo* and stay the wrath the ancestor spirits would hold for anyone who had betrayed them? In all this mystery, in this land of exile, where might a newcomer turn for surety or counsel?

metaphysical insurance

Because these kinds of questions persisted during all the years they toiled in the canefields, many Islanders took the metaphysical insurance of planting their herbs near the canefields and remembering the *akalo* in out-of-work rituals. And just as some of the island herbs adapted to the new country and can still be found clumped in tropical Queensland gullies, so have many actions, meanings, legacies and stories of the Islanders insinuated the landscape too. Like several other communities that have left traces in the Capricorn badlands, the Melanesian labour-recruits learned to live with strife tempering daily life in a place where Death regularly produced ancestors and endless future obligations rather than the finitude and ascension that European religion espoused.

Accordingly, today, several generations after the labour ships have stopped coming, all the Islander deaths that are past and remembered here have mixed in with all the troubles that shocked the badlands during the first years when the Darambal watched the white strangers arrive. Many contemporary Australians feel compelled to deny the Islanders any ancestral status in a comfortable modern federation. (The Islanders presently seem to be even further down the political agenda than Aboriginal rights.) There is a tendency to ignore all the scrappy memories of past exploitations in Australia, to say that they are now so little in evidence that they have no bearing on the present. But because the Melanesians lived and died in the world we have inherited, because they laboured in a deathly process that has been systematically yet unsuccessfully ignored in popular memory, and because their presence still resonates in descendants and community tales, in photographs and gravestones, and in lingering dynasties of wealth, they are part of the world we take our living from.

Like stockman Jemmy and all the other people Frederick Wheeler murdered, like every community dispossessed or exploited during the pioneer years and the squatting decades, the Melanesians were something the beneficiaries of colonialism could not face. A habit of denial thus became endemic in colonial mentality. Over time, the habit has grown into a fearful reflex of withdrawal from the customary, communal practices of witnessing and historical reflection.

But a national mentality need not remain so constrained, particularly when one realises that attentiveness to the past and its peoples can be practical and self-serving. No matter how the persisting memories might get evoked — in families, in books, letters, graves or photos — they can offer ways to acknowledge and incorporate (rather than fearfully exclude) all the heterogeneous peoples and experiences that comprise the past and constitute the present and future of a polyglot nation. To acknowledge a full array of memories is to bring contentious differences into the body politic, to know these differences willingly and inventively rather than with dread or melancholy.

Habits such as fear and denial don't get wished away. Nor do they atrophy through being ignored. They need to be dispersed by the work of close analysis, emotional realisation and rituals of acceptance. We cannot hope to take instruction from the deaths and ructions in the Australian past until we understand why some sectors of the Australian populace have continued to need their badlands, their places of disappearance and denial. Which means we need to understand what went wrong during the decades after Federation, when the violence subtending the colony was fearfully and forcefully ignored to the extent that the habit of denial became a national characteristic.

PRESENTLY

Version 7

Melancholy State

In March 1904, the recently federated Australian parliament outlawed the use of indentured labour in tropical agriculture. This was part of an administrative regime that became known as the 'White Australia Policy'. During the previous forty years, more than sixty thousand Islanders had lived and toiled to make the wealth of the Queensland sugar country. Up to a quarter of them had died there too, leaving a myriad graves and mortuary legends. Now the Islanders were to be removed from national experience. Deportation orders were served on all the black canecutting communities. They had to be gone by the end of 1906.

But Melanesian-Australian culture would not be so perfunctorily expunged. At least two thousand stayed on covertly after the deportation deadline, eventually becoming the forebears of tens of thousands of descendants now living all over Australia. Even so, it is undeniable that the Commonwealth had tried to negate the Australian reality of the Islanders. A xenophobic communal tendency had now been set by parliamentary decree. With the turning of the century, British Australians were officially stricken sick with an overwhelming anxiety about all non-British presence in the country. In setting the standards for a new nation, white people assumed they were right to disenfranchise any human nature other than their own.

As the twentieth century unfolded, decade by decade, waves of Italian, Maltese, Greek, Baltic and Vietnamese migrants came into Central Queensland. With each influx, the newcomers encountered resentment and resistance from the incumbents. Repeatedly, immigrants have suffered outbursts of violence in this territory, inflicted within their own communities, enacted by others, or thundering out of the sea and sky. But fundamentally it was during the 1900s that past injustices and embitterments, governmental policies and endemic climatic turbulence all coalesced to become socially determinant, to guarantee that disquiet would long prevail in the country north of the Tropic of Capricorn.

Knowing the intercultural collisions and collusions in tropical Queensland, knowing how many people resisted and survived the land-grabbing and exploitation, it seems absurd nowadays to expect the society around the Horror Stretch (or anywhere else in Australia) to accede to a decree and become peaceably and exclusively 'white'. However, in those anxious times of

Federation, proponents of the 'White Australia' policy sought to deny the legitimacy of the several 'hybridities' that had always developed whenever immigrant cultures met on colonised ground.

The 'White Australia Policy' was not a debate about vague abstractions. Flesh and blood and ordinary, every-day lives were being abused and refused. Consider, for example, all the generations of commingling that had occurred in the brothel district of Mackay. Between the 1860s and the early 1900s, racial bans on association were irrelevant in the bordellos, provided money was involved. Famous for its Japanese prostitutes, 'Yoka-hama Lane' was also known as 'Mutton Alley', so there is nothing to romanticise in remembering this place. But here, at least, you might have seen plain examples of all the border breaches and category redefinitions that colonialism causes regardless of how fervently an 'executive' culture might want to exclude them. In the Mackay shantytown, one might have seen Chinese and German gold-sluicers deciding whether to fight each other or trade drunken songs. Melanesian men might have been test-firing Snider rifles they'd just bought at the docks. An Aboriginal bugler from the local Native Police might have been heard playing 'The Rose of Tralee' as he dawdled from eating-house to opium den. And it's likely the whorehouses occasionally hosted the district's most unusual pair of bushrangers: an African-American ex-goldrusher called Henry Ford and William Chambers, an Aborigine famed for his riding skills, both of whom became the subjects of several tavern songs during the brief stint of their notoriety. White men would have been wandering about Yokahama Lane also, inspecting the women who hailed from several parts of the world and waited at skewiff windows and doorways. (Sometimes Aboriginal women worked the far end of the street, but they were always barred from the whorehouses.)

In this 'impure' context, people came together to produce a little wealth at the cost of wounds, deaths and enmities, but they also produced ideas, new habits and progeny. All the brusque and ingenious heterogeneity of colonialism caused invention, negotiation and an ardent, unpredictable sense of a new world constantly emerging. But the administrators of White Australia refused this protean world.

ethical murk

The Islanders' repatriation was one of the ways a fearful Australia was inaugurated, as a nation that could not trust the dynamics that were already inside it. From the time the first canecutters had arrived in Queensland, the state government had vacillated about their value and future within the larger community. Throughout the 1880s and 1890s, the opposing candidates for parliamentary leadership, McIlwraith and Griffith, wooed various voting blocs for and against the labour trade. On one side powerful men in the sugar industry demanded the continuation of the profitable traffic in cheap proletariat. Adversarially, trade unionists were increasingly strident in opposing the aliens who were perceived to be undercutting the wages of 'true Australians'. Furthermore, many citizens were perturbed to compare the Queensland plantations with the Confederacy of American states where slavery and the resulting schism of the Civil War had caused a catastrophe. During the early frontier years in Queensland, the white people had struggled nervously, and often with a conscious sense of guilt, to defeat the Aborigines and later to impede the fortunes of the Chinese who followed close behind the pioneers. National Federation as it was proposed for the turn of the century might have offered some rites of passage out of this ethical murk. However, with the inauguration of the national parliament, the legislators inaugurated and ratified an exclusive European-Australia. Entire aspects of the polyglot past were thus supposed to be erased. The desire for an untainted national reputation and the fledgling labour movement's increasing vigilance about the security of local workers won out over whatever economic benefits might have been flowing to a few planters and millers north of the Tropic of Capricorn.

Hence the deportation of the Islanders and the rejection of plans to replace them in the canefields with Ceylonese 'coolies'. Hence the virtual cessation of Chinese immigration. Hence the programmatic denial of citizenship and homelands for Aboriginal people. And hence the continual arguments, commencing in 1891 when Italian immigrants began to work on the sugar farms, about whether Mediterranean peoples were so swarthy as to be non-European.

the shadow of denial

Threatened by so much apparent contamination, many nationalists felt compelled to segregate and expel all foreign matter from the new state. By advocating such a purge, apologists of White Australia promoted a dream of Australian purity and simplicity, a dream that was radically different from the actual complexities of daily experience still remembered in the recently colonised landscapes that comprised the new nation. The White Australia dreamers tried to believe that a past so recently tumultuous and polyglot could be gone simply by disregarding it.

The histories of most nations founded on violence suggest that an inability or refusal to acknowledge the past will produce evermore confusing and distressing symptoms in the body politic. In the wishful shelter of ignorance or amnesia, an abiding melancholy tends to creep into the populace. Or equally disabling, the society can succumb to a paranoid urge to expunge all dissenting persons and memories. To combat these afflictions, 'post-traumatic' societies can develop techniques of mourning so that the denials might cease, so that guilt and threat might be 'lived out', and citizens might start to earn some kind of worldly wisdom, scars and all. When such 'rehabilitation' is performed successfully, a populace can begin to feel settled and self-determining in the aftermath of the violence that created the society.

Some of this prognosis is derived from social psychologists and historians who have analysed the everyday life of contemporary Germany. Without assuming an easy comparison between Australian colonialism and the German holocaust, one can discern some shared 'rationales' behind the systems of violence that occurred in each situation.

The writing of Margarete and Alexander Mitscherlich is crucial in this respect. In *Society without the Father* and *The Inability to Mourn*, they have argued that the generations who inherited Germany after the catastrophe of World War II 'continue to live in the shadow of denial and repression of events that cannot be undone by acts of forgetting'. As Eric Santner explained the Mitscherlich thesis, the post-traumatic population of Germany 'inherited not guilt so much as the denial of guilt, not losses so much as lost opportunities to mourn losses'. These postwar generations knew that 'damage, loss [and] disorientation' formed their world, but they were not equipped with the techniques for acknowledging the full extent of psychological and cultural complexity their everyday lives now had to encompass.

In the late 1960s, applying a bold diagnostic conceit, the Mitscherlichs began to examine *communal* neuroses by psychoanalysing an *individual* German archetype. They concentrated on a type of patient they were encountering regularly in their therapeutic practices: a person paralysed by *angst*, adrift in an unremitting melancholy. The Mitscherlichs hypothesised that they were encountering a nationwide breakdown in 'ego-development' and that this social malaise was being produced, to a significant degree, by history. Reviewing their therapeutic precepts, the Mitscherlichs focussed on a phase of psychological development known as 'infantile narcissism'. During this transitionary interlude, in the 'normal' course of a German person's development, the subject is goaded into growth by learning, through daily experiment, that a mature person encounters many experiences which challenge and outreach the knowledge and wishes of any single, infantile ego. Thus a social consciousness begins to grow. Like a child who is 'less intent on sharing in the feelings of the other person than on confirming its own self-esteem', an 'infantile' or 'narcissistic' ego is wrapped up in its own needs. But a mature individual (and, by extension, a healthy society comprised of such citizens) attains composure firstly by sensing his or her own incompleteness and then by realising that the real world does not merely serve or reflect the self-absorbed, needy ego. Consequent to this realisation, the maturing subject commences a process of mourning the loss of that infantile paradise in which the world seemed to mirror all urges and needs, in which the world seemed to exist only because the infant existed.

Grief, pain and panic will seize the maturing ego when it confronts the complexity and seeming intractability of the adult world. Thus the mourning commences, but if the subject can be successfully guided through such trauma, s/he can begin to see the benefits of relinquishing the fantasy of a simple, self-affirmative world. During this 'mourning work', the subject begins to shape an existence better attuned to objective reality. Through processes of 'realisation' nurtured by a cohesive family and by social regimes of tuition and support, one can participate at last in the complex dynamics of social and historical obligation. The maturing subject need no longer feel compelled to shelter from actuality in delusion, or denial, or selfish intransigence whenever the world does not confirm all selfish needs or desires. Thus one can be emboldened to abandon narcissism and learn how differences between oneself and others can be embraced as enrichment rather than threat.

If this mourning does not occur, a person cannot venture into actuality. Unable to acknowledge the real world around them, terminal narcissists retreat to fantasies which the larger world will constantly discredit. Thus the immature ego can get stalled in unending melancholy, or perhaps even in a catatonia of denial that must be protected endlessly by wilful amnesia and stasis.

When people get trapped like this in narcissism, they crave a world containing no perplexity, no otherness or uncanniness contradicting a self-affirming world. Klaus Theweleit's celebrated study of *Male Fantasies* makes this point in relation to the repetitive, metallic images of the military machine and the uniformed, faceless warrior that were fetishes for Nazi ideologues. The Nazi subject demanded to see nothing but an endless array of itself massed as a profusion of identical elements. The Nazis strove to produce a narcissist nation — they wanted an entire, invariant world of Teutonic sameness — and despite the eventual demolition of the Reich, they appeared to have left such a populace adrift in the aftermath.

A narcissistic subject feels compelled to think in a rigid, bipolar fashion: either everyone outside oneself is reflective and exactly *like* oneself, or they are disorderly and *different* and must be made nonexistent. Inclusion versus exclusion. For the stranded ego, 'strangeness' can be comprehended only as a threat, as something self-negating. Thus the eradication of difference becomes a fearful, compulsive response. There can be no negotiation on a 'middle ground', no compromise or preparedness to change as the result of an exchange. All things unlike oneself must be refused as uncanny because they do not reflect and affirm the dream-ofwholeness which was conjured in the infantile, world-comprising relationship of mother-and-infant. The narcissist (and the Nazi) is terminally nostalgic, craving that infantile paradise, refusing any other possible world.

the passage to independence

Tracking the Mitscherlichs' rationale, we can see how Nazi Germany was at first a society 'stranded' by the losses of the First World War. In the wake of this trauma, Germans became 'fixated' on the figure of Hitler, who contrived to present himself as the dutiful, narcissistic son of Mother Germany. Hitler's triumph, his great, mythic sleight of mind, was that he and Germany were perceived as the same. During the 1930s, the German people 'identified' with Hitler and sought to exclude all otherness through the purge of holocaust. This was an extremist politic of nostalgia.

Once Nazism had failed, the German populace attempted to forget that such a purge had really happened. This was the purge of the purge — an extremist politic of amnesia. But because the outside world did not 'ratify' these fantastic denials of reality, and because the majority of the people had identified so entirely with Hitler, many postwar psyches were trapped in the blasted shelter of their narcissism. They were incapable of acknowledging a world that had refused the Reich, yet they could no longer admire their Nazi self-image even as they were unable to abjure it.

The Mitscherlichs maintain that the wounds in the German psyche can be cured only if a double mourning process is undertaken: firstly the people must admit that the holocaust was caused by their own inability to include otherness in their ethos; and secondly they need to acknowledge that every generation since the war has hidden futilely in igorance by avoiding the traumas of self-analysis now that the Final Solution has been proven a perfidious fact and a failure. For the majority of the German populace, melancholic self-abasement has been the outcome. Alternatively, in a smaller faction, an increasingly strident regime of exclusion, in the form of neo-Nazism, has arisen with an evermore fearful and fierce rejection of any identity different from the national-socialist fantasy of ethnic purity. As Thomas Elsaesser has summarised the Mitscherlichs' argument, 'the German nation ... would have to undertake collective "mourning work", making an acknowledgement of loss and of separation from the love object', or narcissistic fixation, which had been embodied by Hitler and all that he represented as the fantasm of a singular, eternal Germany. The post-traumatic society can hope to 'make the passage to independence' only by 'reliving and restaging the ambivalences of primary narcissism: the rage and anger of abandonment, and the desire for merging and doubling'. If the parent generation failed to make this passage, 'the problems would return to haunt the children'.

seeping blood

The Mitscherlichs' model of social melancholy can be usefully applied to the *colonial* mentality, prompting speculation that a colony might attain maturity only when it learns to include an array of ethnic, psychological, sexual and political differences in its constitution. According to this model, a maturing colony cannot take shelter in a narcissistic, exclusive fixation on its likeness to the mother country.

Of course, no-one can sanely claim that the Final Solution is neatly analogous to the processes of violence, exploitation and exclusion that convulsed Australia during the frontier times and the ensuing decades of settlement. However, the comparison forces us to confront the fact of attempted genocide in Australia's recent history. It also helps isolate some causes of Australia's abiding social ills. It helps us assay the 'ghosts' that so many people glimpse in the Australian landscape nowadays.

This 'haunting' is not only metaphorical. It is a way to name a perturbance that lingers in the Australian consciousness. At the time of Federation, significant portions of Australian society were grievous and melancholy. Which is to say that several communities struggled and stalled in their mourning-work as they attempted to form a mature entity integrated under the name of one nation. The White Australia Policy can be interpreted, in part, as a melancholic refusal to allow differences into the definition of the society. The newly federated nation, confronted with the paradoxical opportunity-and-threat of maturity in the complicated world, could not 'let go' of its fixation on Mother England. The legislature demanded that similitude with England be the defining characteristic of its populace. Hence the White Australia Policy. This insistence was a way to avoid the mourning which could have caused painful acknowledgments which would in turn have led to the unending creation of a dynamic and heterogeneous national identity.

Moreover, in that *fin-de-siecle* time, one further technique was used to distract attention from the past: political rhetoric emphasised the need to concentrate on the *future* tasks of nation-building. In this instance, the German experience is instructive again, most cogently in Thomas Elsaesser's description of the communal distraction-techniques that were enacted in the postwar German republic to ensure that history remained unacknowledged:

> Instead of confronting this past, Germans preferred to bury it … the frantic reconstruction and rebuilding effort known as the economic miracle was sustained not only

by the Marshall Plan and NATO defences, but by the psychological defences as well. These help to explain why the work ethic and the ideologies of effort and self-sacrifice played such an important part in German family life.

Comparably, in Australia, during the Federation times and the years leading up to the spectacular self-sacrifices of Gallipoli, people turned their attention to dramas of valiant battling, both in the domestic development of primary industries for trade and in the international theatres of warfare and sporting endeavour. Each of these huge rituals involved a 'reflexive' identification with Britain. Each had the desired effects firstly of distracting citizens from the unsettling remains of the previous century, and secondly of directing Australians' attention to the suspenseful, engrossing struggle for future security and/or prosperity.

mock the boundaries

This focussing of attention can be understood as social narcissism, and Central Queensland experienced an intensified version of it. Deporting the Islanders from the canegrowing regions was part of an explicit, national refusal to know the legacies of recent history. However, in the same way that federal deportation-agents soon realised that it would be impossible to locate and remove many of the other races who had become part of the

Central Queensland landscape — the Chinese, the Japanese, the Aboriginal survivors, the Javanese, the Ceylonese, as well as the southern Italians and Sicilians who had just begun to arrive — so it also grew obvious that the Melanesian presence would never be completely expunged. At the very least, the stories of the Islanders' Central Queensland lives would persist in popular consciousness. The disquieting history of the Islanders' exploitation and death would always burr away at any mentalities who wished to claim that Australia was a rightfully white and integrated European community, pure and simple.

During the forty years before Federation, thousands of Melanesian labourers had seeped into the Queensland society after their indenture terms had finished. Many time-expired Islanders from the Mackay environs wandered and worked far from the sugarfields. Often they boarded steamers up and down the coast, scrounging work in other canefields or recruiting on pearling steamers with Japanese and Aboriginal crewmates. Other times they would walk hundreds of kilometres following gossip and clues in quest of friends and relatives who had been assigned to faraway plantations. In the context of White Australia, such nomadism threatened to mock the boundaries, categories and regulations with which the nation was defining itself so cleanly.

In Central Queensland, white supremacists could make an especially long list of contaminants they needed to expunge: all the miscegenations that sullied the anglican gene pool; the 'Kanaka Pidgin English' which was stammering the mother tongue (even as it allowed profitable regimes of trade and labour to function) in the canefields and the mills; the runaway canecutters who were living in the bush, often communing with Aborigines and Chinese who were also struggling and negotiating on the margins of the white settlements; the Malay and Singhalese workers who had absconded over the years and persisted 'in direct competition with the white man', as the *Mackay Standard* had declared in 1883; the backsliding farmers who had befriended their indentured workers and were allowing time-expired Islanders to tend fields covertly, usually by moonlight, to avoid detection and reprisals from the strengthening union movement which vigorously discouraged non-European labour in the major industries. Despite the wishes of apologists for White Australia, therefore, it was obvious an unregulated 'promiscuity' of categories was occurring in the tropics. The extirpation of otherness in Central Queensland seemed futile, but instead of accepting the 'unruliness' of the cultures along the Capricorn hinterland, governmental law and popular lore described a landscape where everything causing anxiety could be consigned to a zone of 'irrationality'. Thus arose the image of the central Queensland badlands, a no-go area for White Australia, a tract which, like the dead centre, could be cordoned off from sociability and everyday consciousness; a tract of Australia which was paradoxically and usefully not-Australia.

---

traffic with aliens

The Weckert killings, in 1975, are perhaps the most notorious outburst from the badlands in recent memory. The fact that the homicides happened *in that place* and were reported so fervidly *at that particular time* is no accident. The murders of these outsiders, performed and narratively set as they were in this alienated and anxious region, have a mythic aspect in the way the slayings distil some basic, topical terror of itinerancy and foreignness. During the 1970s, a pluralist Australia was beginning to assert itself just as the isolationist and exclusive 'Anglo' nation was losing credibility. Regarding the Horror Stretch, the murders in the 1960s and 1970s — both their actual occurrence and their compulsively frequent re-narrating — can be interpreted as symptoms flaring at precisely the time when the old 'ailment' of White Australia was most under attack. The murders and their mythic re-tellings represented a fever of xenophobia arising just when the disease was being purged.

This word 'mythic' … there are countless ways to understand it. I want to define it this way: a myth is a popular story that highlights contradictions which a community feels compelled to resolve *narratively* rather than rationally, so that citizens can get on with living. Myths help us live with contradictions, whereas histories help us analyse persistent contradictions so that we might avoid being lulled and ruled by the myths that we use to console and enable ourselves. Which is why we desire our myths and need our histories.

In these respects, the 'Weckert version' of the badlands legend is mythic. The stories of the killings were told and re-told so as to raise and resolve contemporary anxieties about the expiry of White Australia. By the mid-1970s, multiculturalism and the end of economic protectionism were becoming a fact and a destiny in national life. This meant that a kind of 'otherness' now had to be acknowledged as abounding and ineradicable within the nation. The Weckert murders seized the popular imagination because they prompted stories about a pressing national contradiction: old Australian beliefs have always contended that it is dangerous to traffic with aliens, yet citizens were obliged now to share rights and responsibilities with others.

The Weckerts drove in like mythic templates for all these concerns. They were outsiders: Sophie was originally from Germany, Noel from South Australia. The night they died, they had come down from the Far North, camping in their car like swaggies. On the Stretch they were obviously alien.

Now add the killers, who were outsiders too. As their characteristics took and shifted shape during the period of the manhunt, the killers were phantoms, possibly black, possibly prison escapees. Certainly they were invisible and ubiquitous in the fearful consciousness of a populace that demanded their capture. All these strangers met in a zone characterised as ungovernable by a century of storytelling. When the three culprits were finally charged, they were found to be roustabouts and circus-hands, of no fixed address, originally from Tasmania, the Far South. So much rootlessness — the Weckerts, the roustabouts, this latitude with all its meteorological turbulence — and so much alienation came together along this Stretch, this place that has been known for so long as simultaneously unworldly and part of the Australian homeland.

If the Weckert story was a typical badland tale, what was its mythic function? In part it helped the teller and the listener acknowledge that instability and contentious strains of difference or 'otherness' were abroad in the community, coursing through the perturbed nation. The story allowed the tellers and the listeners to acknowledge their anxieties about nomadism and incursive foreignness. Locating the slayings in a voidland which had long been cordoned off and understood to be unlike the rest of the well-husbanded continent, the Weckert myth dramatised a crucial contradiction of contemporary Australian experience: xenophobia was still widespread at the same time as people knew that the extirpation of foreignness was no longer valid in a society that was finally opening itself to the world

172

of cultural and economic diversity. People needed stories such as the Weckert legend to help them live with these kinds of contradictions. It was a story about losing the dream of a protected, stable economy in a settled, uniform Anglo-Australia. Citizens were dreading change and refusing it, but they also knew it to be inevitable.

The *event* of the Weckert murders was produced by more than the mood of the times, but the *story* and its avid consumption and circulation were overwhelmingly a product of communal sentiment. The story bloomed and grew popular because people seized on it and offered it to each other in a needful mood. The story quickly became a myth.

In the workings of badland myth, the very fact that a special 'quarantine-zone' exists within a general location tends to guarantee that everywhere else outside the cordon can be defined (with reference to the no-go zone) as well-regulated, social and secure. When telling a Horror Stretch story, a narrator can give the impression that anxieties about evil have not been ignored or repressed. And in the same breath, while acknowledging that dysfunction is abroad, the narrator can also show that trouble can be assigned to a no-go area, to a place which is comprehensible as elsewhere-but-still-in-Australia. Thus citizens can feel well-counselled to stay out of the badlands, to glimpse but then ignore the trouble humming in there, and get on with living.

This is a powerfully mythic use of the Capricornian landscape.

---

worry away

Developing an *historical* understanding of the landscape, on the other hand, teaches us to worry away at our myths even as they lull us into not worrying. In quiet times for the badlands (for example, the uneventful years after the upgrading of Highway One during the late 1980s), when fewer stories flare and circulate, you begin to wonder if the society needs such a mythic badland anymore. You wonder if people have begun to know their places differently and inclusively. You hope that the society has overcome the habits of repression and denial that badland stories tend to serve. You become hopeful, for if we have learned how to mourn the inequities and losses in our past, we have probably also learned how to deserve our landscapes, how to take instruction from them and all their previous custodians. Under such conditions the badlands could cease to exist, not because they have been fully controlled, but because they no longer have topical meaning *as badlands*. In such a new era, citizens might know themselves and their environments maturely, diversely and extensively. Knowledge rather than fear might be the emotion governing the landscape. This would be a time when people could know themselves *in* their place rather than in spite of it, a time when the badlands get lost in the profuse negotiations of everyday life, a time at last when difference and change can be welcomed rather than quarantined.

But until this maturity is completely achieved, until the fantasy of one simple, singular nation is dispatched and the fear of difference is overcome, the hybrid vitality in our places and peoples will be wasted. Our landscapes will continue to go bad on us and we will continue to make legends from them.

You hope never to hear a new Horror Stretch myth. But you look at the history of the place and its surrounds, and you brace yourself for the next episode.

Who shall heal murder? what is done is done.
Go forth! fulfil thy days! and be thy deeds
Unlike the last!

George Gordon, Lord Byron, *Cain*

Exit

When I started contemplating the Horror Stretch, I presumed I was on a private quest to know a worthless stretch of scrubby floodplain. But before long, the quest became an inquest. So I've been tracking this landscape for a while now, this world of trouble and stark beauty. To account for its complexities, I've tried to see its landmarks better, to know the physical environment, to understand its vastness, its climatic outbursts and errant ecologies.

I've learned that the Capricorn hinterland behaves like a live thing, naturally present and always evolving — a creature animated by its own powers. It is *land*, the organism that contains all other organisms. It is something vigorous and primeval, therefore, something outstretching human control and interpretation. But it is also an ever-assembling mosaic of cultural artefacts, relics and stories that people have left on and in the ground. More than solely natural, the region is perhaps best understood as *country*, a notion encompassing nature and human obligation that white Australia has learned slowly from Indigenous Australia.

My inquest on the Horror Stretch has gone to strikingly different locations. I've journeyed back and forth from glaring, grey cattle-country around Rockhampton in the south, to lambent, green sugar-country between Mackay and Bowen in the north. Combing through court reports, journals, legends, history books, maps and photographs, I've run my reading and writing through many variations of tone and genre, rather like the experience of driving the highway that insinuates the Stretch.

Crossing and re-crossing this unruly country, I've looked for messages in patterns formed by land-use and migration, in stories associated with creek-beds, weed-patches and gravestones. And the closer I've looked, the more the place has come into focus as a mythological badland, a paradoxically real and fantastic location where malevolence is *simply there* partly because it has long been *imagined there*.

Why does some country get called bad? Partly it's because the law needs the outlaw for reassuring citizens that the unruly and the unknown can be named and contained even if they cannot be annihilated. Their function is to acknowledge but also to deny insufficiencies that are part of everyday social and psychic reality. Perhaps you know of a place close to your home, some 'wrong' suburb alongside a rail line, a no-go house or park around the corner where something dreadful is said to have concussed the spirit of the environment. Such places are badlands. Some of them are not places you can drive or walk to. For a badland can exist inside your own consciousness, in the past perhaps, or in caches of denial shoved to the back of the mind.

Regardless of where or when they get located, though, badlands eventually demand our attention, because their perimeters are rarely secure. The troubles we'd like to contain 'over there' tend to turn up repeatedly in our own lived experience. Our badlands are vital because they can disturb us into recognising the issues that we wish we could deny, ignore or forget.

Forgetting simply does not work. Wishful amnesia is no protection against memories of actual, lived experience. The events of the past rarely pass. They leave marks in documents, in bodies, in communities and places, in buildings, streets and landscapes. People insist on remembering the events that have made their lives. When people remember, they take part in stories prompted by marks, traces and places. In remembrance people strive to know events in their entirety, abhorring denials and erasures. To remember effectively, people need to recall the entire pattern of the past, including the failings and futilities. To deny the entirety of a story is usually to refuse difficulty, to wish away dif-

ference or contradiction. From such refusal melancholy
looms.

---

a broil of kitchen-workers

One of the ways I remember tropical Queensland is
from the summers I drudged as a teenaged civilian
cook hired in to cosset explosive kerosene stoves in
army camps whenever troops went on manouevres in
the bush around Rockhampton. This was the early
1970s. Initially, the whopping overtime rates plus the
living-away-from-home stipends and danger-money
were the only attractions of such an arduous job. In
tented kitchen compounds, we spent stifling weeks
working and drinking and entertaining each other between bouts of irritability that occasionally flared into
outright enmity. But as the summers came and went,
I began to appreciate something else about the job:
the way a broil of kitchen-workers always develop an
argumentative accommodation of different ethnicities
and experiences. In the abrasive scrub, with everyone
pressure-cookered together, toleration was always the
best way to survive a forty-day bivouac.

It was in the bush kitchen that I got to know Tony
Zammitt, an astonishingly strong Maltese man from
Bowen who had spent his adult life grafting for odd-jobs
up and down the Queensland coast. Tony could drink

and swear and toil and bludge in ways most people have never even considered. But like many of the men who worked the camps, he could also amaze you with the tenderness of his soul. One night we were scrubbing the huge cooking pots — 'Dixie-bashing' it's called by cooks everywhere in the English-speaking world. Between swigs of high-proof lemon essence we'd snaffled from the Q-store on a ruse that we were going to make curd tarts, Tony sang a breathtakingly beautiful lament in Maltese. When I asked him what the song meant, he avoided an explanation for a while but eventually said that it was about being *surrounded*, that it concerned the way people live on an island, the way the Maltese have learned to keep their secrets and to treasure their knowledge. He said this with the grin that usually signalled a fiction, then offered a drunken motto:

Tell no secrets on the sea-shore. Declare no love, no schemes of vengeance. Take no oath along the beachfront. For the sea-shells hear everything and keep all the messages. And shells always whisper to any vagabond who bends down to listen.

This memory of Tony — plunging his huge arms elbow-deep in suds and drunkenly incanting — connects with my memories of the road-ghosts and the preacher whom I encountered as a ten-year-old in the back seat of my parents' car. Tony's motto seems perfectly attuned to the history of migration, fear, yearning and nervous accommodation that has been played out repeatedly all over the badlands of Central Queensland.

---

bend down to listen

I heard Tony's voice replay in my head thirty years later when I revisited the sugar country where some of us cooks used to sneak off occasionally when we knew we wouldn't be missed for a half-day. Out behind the old graveyard at Sarina, just south of Mackay, a quiet road runs easterly through the canefields to the sea. After driving for twenty minutes, you can ease your car down a side track to a beach that's littered with talkative shells. How much colonial toil has gone into this country! How many island peoples have sat down on this beach in an hour's respite from the canefields or the railroad-construction gangs! Greeks. Sicilians. Maltese. Japanese. Scots. Irish. Malaitans. English. Tannese. Guadalcanalans. Singhalese. There were the Tamils too, originally from South Hindustan, who fled to Ceylon in the 1880s and then enlisted to dive for pearls off the coast of North Queensland. In the off-season, they made their way down to Mackay to crush sugar cane in the new mills. New Guinea men followed a similar path. Then came Filipinos speaking Malay and Spanish and Pidgin English. Javanese too.

All these horizon-watchers, all with their own rules

for an islander's survival. All these people talking in their dialects, telling stories and singing songs. What a world of trouble and yearning the shells on this isolated beach have heard. What a resonant piece of country we're on the edge of. If you stand here and squint a little, the mood of the place thickens and the shells themselves speak up. Sometimes they offer the murmur of a lullaby, other times a deafening war cry. And if you listen carefully and resist the urge to get away from the eeriness that's closing in, you might fancy you can hear the shells whispering a thousand words for 'home' every time a wave washes out.

Reading behind the Versions

Sources of Quotations

page 2 — Daoist motto from Gary Snyder, *The Practice of the Wild*, San Francisco: North Point Press, 1990, p. 126.

page 12 — 'the weather ... to move' from George Randall, 'Log Report' regarding the cyclone at Flat Top light and signalling station, Mackay, January 1918, in Mackay Historical Society *Bulletin* no. 8, 1972, p. 6.

page 16 — 'It is ... to reign' from Charles Sturt, *Two Expeditions into the Interior of Southern Australia, during the years 1828, 1829, 1830, and 1831*, 2 vols, London: Smith, Elder and Co., 1833, vol. 2, p. 59.

page 50 — 'in the ... mythology' from Ernst Cassirer, *The Philosophy of Symbolic Forms, vol. 2: Mythical Thought*, New Haven: Yale University Press, 1955, p. 5.

page 56 — 'hauling over' — see L.E. Skinner, *Police of the Pastoral Frontier; Native Police 1849–59*, St Lucia: University of Queensland Press, 1975, p. 355. Skinner cites snippets of Wheeler's reports, which can be found in the 'Files of the Colonial Secretary's Office of New South Wales' in the John Oxley Library, Brisbane. See particularly, microfilm reel A2/41, for the year 1858.

page 57 — Wheeler report — see letter from F Wheeler, Marlborough, to Commissioner of Police, August 1, 1872, Queensland State Archives, Col/A170, letter 1484 of 1872 file, cited in Raymond Evans, Kay Saunders and Kathryn Cronin, *Exclusion, Exploitation and Extermination: Race Relations in Colonial Queensland*, Sydney: Australian and New Zealand Book Co., 1975, p. 50.

page 61 — 'race and … communities' from Henry Reynolds, *Frontier: Aborigines, Settlers and Land*, Sydney: Allen and Unwin, 1987, p. 193.

page 62 — 'not so … ponderable' from Tim Rowse, 'Mabo and Moral Anxiety', *Meanjin*, vol. 52, no. 2 (1993), p. 229.

page 63 — 'the atrocities … ages' — quoted in Gordon Reid, *A Nest of Hornets: The massacre of the Fraser family at the Hornet Bank Station, Central Queensland, 1857, and related events*, Melbourne: Oxford University Press, 1982, p. 186.

page 63 — 'Dispossession … injustices' from Justices Deane and Gaudron, High Court of Australia, 'Eddie Mabo and Ors and the State of Queensland', Court's reasons for judgment, typescript, 1992, p. 100, quoted by Rowse, 'Mabo', p. 235.

page 65 — 'Were it ... dismissal' from R.R. Mackenzie, 'Chairman's Report', *The Select Committee on the Native Police Force and the Conditions of the Aborigines in General*, Queensland Legislative Assembly, 1861. The 'Report' and transcriptions of interviews with witnesses, including Wheeler himself, are extensively excerpted in Bill Rosser, *Up Rode the Troopers: The Black Police in Queensland*, St Lucia: University of Queensland Press, 1990, pp. 167–204.

page 65 — 'It was ... place' — Report from Wheeler to Lt J. Murray, Commander of the Port Curtis and Leichhardt Division of the Native Police, October 17, 1858, quoted in Skinner, *Police of the Pastoral Frontier*, p. 355.

page 78 — 'fond of ... words' from Carl Lumholtz, *An Account of Four Years' Travels in Australia and of Camp Life with the Aborigines of Queensland*, New York: Charles Scribner's Son, 1889, p. 49.

page 78 — 'the white Mary' from Lorna McDonald, *Rockhampton: A History of City and District*, St Lucia: University of Queensland Press, 1981, p. 188.

page 78 — 'shot while ... to escape' from J. Grant Pattison, *Battlers' Tales of Early Rockhampton*, Melbourne: Fraser & Jenkinson, 1939, pp. 98–100, and McDonald, *Rockhampton*, pp. 188–89.

page 81 — 'what we're ... mourning' from Michael Lesy,

The Forbidden Zone, London: Picador, 1988, pp. 233–34.

page 82 — 'I began ... the living' from Stephen Greenblatt, *Shakespearean Negotiations: The Circulation of Social Energy in Renaissance England*, Berkeley: University of California Press, 1988, p. 1. See also ' "Intensifying the surprise as well as the school": Stephen Greenblatt interviewed by Noel King', in *Textual Practice* Vol. 8, No. 1 (Spring, 1994), pp. 117–18.

pages 83–84 — 'If the ... such cases' quoted in Reid, *A Nest of Hornets,* pp. 166–67.

page 87 — 'Time ran ... we were' from James Morrill, *Sketch of a Residence among the Aboriginals of Northern Queensland for seventeen years*, Brisbane: Courier General Printing Office, 1863, p. 12.

page 96 — 'At sundown ... creek' from John Mackay, 'Captain Mackay's Expedition', a narrative of the expedition to the Pioneer River, first published in the *Armidale Express and Maitland Mercury* and reprinted in Henry Ling Roth, *The Discovery and Settlement of Port Mackay, Queensland*, Halifax: F. King and Sons, 1908, pp. 30–31. Further citations from Mackay's narrative are from pp. 31–38.

page 98 — 'You go ... them' — J.K. Wilson, Votes and Proceedings, Queensland Government, 1861, Doc 479, par 50, cited in Skinner, *Police of the Pastoral Frontier*, p. 372.

page 100 — 'Duke ... heart' from Andrew Murray, 'Journal of an expedition from Uralla, N.S.W. into Queensland to take up new country for grazing, 31 Dec. 1859–7 Aug. 1860'. Mitchell Library manuscripts, Mss 736 in Microfilm Fm4/3096, p. 38.

page 105 — Noel Loos, *Invasion and Resistance: Aboriginal–European relations on the North Queensland frontier 1861–1897*, Canberra: Australian National University Press, 1982, p. 28. Loos identifies a fourth zone — rainforests — which were important further north than the brigalow.

page 109 — 'It has … Heavenwards' from Edward B. Kennedy, *The Black Police of Queensland Reminiscence of Official Work and Personal Adventures in the Early days of the Colony*, London: John Murray, 1902, pp. 125–26.

pages 121–22 — '25% … drought' from the Introduction to W.E. Giles, *A Cruize in a Queensland Labour Vessel to the South Seas*, edited and introduced by Deryck Scarr, Canberra: Australian National University Press, 1968, p. 22.

page 123 — 'Melange … labels' from Roger Keesing and Peter Corris, *Lightning Meets the West Wind: The Malaita Massacre*, Melbourne: Oxford University Press, 1980, p. 10.

page 125 — 'Major … *mamana*' from Clive Moore, *Kanaka: A History of Melanesian Mackay*, Port Moresby: Institute of Papua New Guinea Studies, 1985, p. 175.

page 131 — 'rolls … stopped' from Keesing and Corris, *Lightning Meets the West Wind*, p. 125.

page 136 — mortality rate — Kay Saunders, 'The Pacific Islander Hospitals In Colonial Queensland', in *Journal of Pacific History*, vol. 11 (1976), pp. 41–42.

page 136 — 'Some ... over then' from ABC Radio 'Broadband' series, *The Forgotten People: a history of the Australian South Sea Island community*, Sydney: ABC, 1979, p. 52.

pages 139–40 — 'the incidents ... islands' from Moore, *Kanaka*, p. 269.

page 142 — 'Killing ... irrational' from Moore, *Kanaka,* p. 75. See also, Keesing and Corris, *Lightning Meets the West Wind,* p. 10.

page 142 — payback — Henry Reynolds, 'The Other Side of the Frontier: Early Aboriginal Reactions to Pastoral Settlement in Queensland and Northern New South Wales', in Henry Reynolds (ed.), *Race Relations in North Queensland*, Townsville: History Dept of James Cook University of North Queensland, 1978, p. 9.

page 144 — 'sleep ... to hand' from Mackay *Mercury*, November 29, 1894, quoted in Moore, *Kanaka*, p. 270.

page 144 — 'made up ... sorcery' from Moore, *Kanaka*, p. 270.

pages 144–45 — 'the Guadalcanal ... happened' from Noel Fatnowna (edited by Roger Keesing), *Fragments of a Lost Heritage*, Sydney: Angus & Robertson, 1989, p. 15.

page 159 — 'continue ... forgettings' from Margarete Mitscherlich, *Erinnerungsarbeit: Zur Pyschoanalyse der Un-*

fahigkeit zu trauern, Frankfurt: S. Fischer, 1987, p. 114, cited and translated by Eric L. Santner, *Stranded Objects: Mourning, Memory and Film in Postwar Germany*, Ithaca: Cornell University Press, 1990, p. 34. See also Alexander Mitscherlich, *Society without the Father: A Contribution to Social Psychology*, London: Tavistock, 1969; and Alexander and Margarete Mitscherlich, *The Inability to Mourn*, London: Tavistock, 1975.

page 159 — 'inherited ... losses' from Eric L. Santner, *Stranded Objects*, p. 34.

page 160 — 'less intent ... self-esteem', from A. and M. Mitscherlich, *The Inability to Mourn*, p. 63.

pages 164–65 — 'the German ... children' from Thomas Elsaesser, *New German Cinema: A History*, London: Macmillan, 1989, p. 242.

pages 166–67 — 'Instead ... family life' from Elsaesser, *New German Cinema*, p. 242.

page 169 — 'indirect ... white man' from *Mackay Standard: Illustrated Christmas Supplement*, 1883, p. 4.

Further Reading

I've read and re-read some fine writing as I've sought guidance across my versions of the badland. For anyone looking to continue the inquest, here are a few texts that might offer some startling perspectives or strange lights.

Landscape

On how landscapes live in human consciousness, two books have been especially sustaining:

> Barry Lopez, *Arctic Dreams: Imagination and Desire in a Northern Landscape*, New York: Charles Scribner's Sons, 1986.

> Gary Snyder, *The Practice of the Wild*, San Francisco: North Point Press, 1990.

For a thorough and occasionally astonishing account of acacia eco-systems in Queensland, I recommend:

> A. Bailey (ed.), *The Brigalow Belt of Australia*, Brisbane: The Royal Society of Queensland, 1984.

The Badlands Motif

For an idiosyncratic account of 'Starkweather fever' and the investiture of the rampager in the mass-media bestiary, see:

> Greil Marcus, *Lipstick Traces: A Secret History of the Twentieth Century*, Cambridge (Mass.): Harvard University Press, 1989.

And with a more local focus, it's always rewarding to trek back through the ur-text of Australian badland iconography:

> Charles Sturt, *Two Expeditions into the Interior of Southern Australia, during the years 1828, 1829, 1830, and 1831*, 2 vols, London: Smith, Elder and Co., 1833.

Native Police in Queensland

For almost thirty years, one study of frontier policing has remained fundamental:

> L.E. Skinner, *Police of the Pastoral Frontier: Native Police 1849–59*, St Lucia: University of Queensland Press, 1975.

Skinner cites snippets of Frederick Wheeler's reports, which can also be found in the 'Files of the Colonial Secretary's Office of New South Wales' in the John Oxley Library, Brisbane. See particularly microfilm reel A2/41 for the year 1858.

Also highly recommended:

> Bill Rosser, *Up Rode the Troopers: The Black Police in Queensland*, St Lucia: University of Queensland Press, 1990.

Rosser has good access to oral-history remembrance about the Native Police and he also provides extensive excerpts from R.R. Mackenzie's 'Chairman's Report' in *The Select Committee on the Native Police Force and the Conditions of the Aborigines in General*, Queensland Legislative Assembly, 1861. Moreover, there are several transcripts of interviews with eyewitnesses of Native Police 'campaigns' and 'dispersals', including passages from Wheeler himself.

For a sanitised memoir which nonetheless has good procedural and logistical details, see:

> Edward B. Kennedy, *The Black Police of Queensland:*

Reminiscence of Official Work and Personal Adventures in the Early days of the Colony, London: John Murray, 1902.

Frontier Realities

As a study in the interlacing 'logics' of frontier life, this book has stood up well to the passing of decades:

Raymond Evans, Kay Saunders and Kathryn Cronin, *Exclusion, Exploitation and Extermination: Race Relations in Colonial Queensland*, Sydney: Australian and New Zealand Book Co., 1975. (Later, UQP edition 1988).

See also:

Barry Morris, 'Frontier Colonialism as a Culture of Terror', in B. Atwood and J. Arnold (eds), *Power, Knowledge, and Aborigines*, special issue of the *Journal of Australian Studies*, no. 35, 1992.

Noel Loos, *Invasion and Resistance: Aboriginal–European relations on the North Queensland frontier 1861–1897*, Canberra: Australian National University Press, 1982.

Massacre Stories

For accounts of 'generic' variants of the hill-slaughter tale see:

David Roberts, 'Bells Falls Massacre and Bathurst's History of Violence: Local Tradition and Australian Historiography', *Australian Historical Studies* 105 (October 1995), pp. 615 – 33.

Clive Moore, 'Blackgin's Leap: A Window into Aboriginal–European Relations in the Pioneer Valley Queensland in the 1960s', *Aboriginal History,* vol. 14, part I (1990), pp. 61 – 79.

Nicola Tareha, *The Legend of the Leap*, Townsville: James Cook University Foundation for Literary Studies, 1986.

For a superb study of the way frontier violence concussed psychologies and reverberated through attitudes and municipal behaviour in Queensland for generations afterwards, see:

Gordon Reid, *A Nest of Hornets: The massacre of the Fraser family at the Hornet Bank Station, Central Queensland, 1857, and related events,* Melbourne: Oxford University Press, 1982.

South Seas Labour Trade

There have been many insightful meditations on the labour trade and its lasting impact in Queensland and the islands. Consider these examples:

Dorothy Shineberg, 'Guns and Men in Polynesia', *The Journal of Pacific History*, vol.6 (1971).

Clive Moore, *Kanaka: A History of Melanesian Mackay*, Port Moresby: Institute of Papua New Guinea Studies, 1985.

Clive Moore, Jacqueline Leckie and Doug Munro (eds), *Labour in the South Pacific*, Townsville: James Cook University Press, 1990.

Roger Keesing and Peter Corris, *Lightning Meets the West Wind: The Malaita Massacre*, Melbourne: Oxford University Press, 1980.

Murray Chapman and R. Mansell Prothero (eds), *Circulation in Population Movement: Substance and Concepts from the Melanesian case*, London: Routledge Kegan Paul, 1985.

Joel Bonnemaison, 'The Tree and the Canoe: Roots and Mobility in Vanuatu Societies', *Pacific Viewpoint*, Vol. 26, no. 1, (1985).

Kay Saunders, 'The Pacific Islander Hospitals In Colonial Queensland', in *Journal of Pacific History*, vol. 11 (1976).

Kay Saunders, 'Melanesian Women in Queensland, 1863–1907: Some Methodological Problems Involving the Relationship between Racism and Sexism', in *Pacific Studies*, vol. 4, no. 1 (1980).

Margaret Jolly, 'The Forgotten Women: A History of Migrant Labour and Gender Relations in Vanuatu', in *Oceania*, vol. 58, no. 2 (1987).

Daniel de Coppet, 'Gardens of Life, Gardens of Death in Melanesia', in *Kabar Seberang*, 8/9 (1981).

Noel Fatnowna (edited by Roger Keesing), *Fragments of a Lost Heritage*, Sydney: Angus & Robertson, 1989.

Patricia Mercer and Clive Moore, 'Melanesians in North Queensland: The Retention of Indigenous Religious and

Magical Practices', in *Journal of Pacific History*, vol. 11 (1976).

Frontier and Settlement Life in Capricornia

Lorna McDonald's study of Rockhampton remains a very impressive work:

Lorna McDonald, *Rockhampton: A History of City and District*, St Lucia: University of Queensland Press, 1981.

For sources much closer to the times, consider the following texts, with their unsettling mix of presumptions, prejudices and directness of declamation:

James Morrill, *Sketch of a Residence among the Aboriginals of Northern Queensland for seventeen years,* Brisbane: Courier General Printing Office, 1863.

Carl Lumholtz, *An Account of Four Years' Travels in Australia and of Camp Life with the Aborigines of Queensland*, New York: Charles Scribner's Son, 1889.

John Mackay, 'Captain Mackay's Expedition', a narrative of the expedition to the Pioneer River, first published in the *Armidale Express and Maitland Mercury*, reprinted in Henry Ling Roth, *The Discovery and Settlement of Port Mackay, Queensland,* Halifax: F. King and Sons, 1908.

Andrew Murray, 'Journal of an expedition from Uralla, N.S.W. into Queensland to take up new country for grazing, 31 Dec. 1859 — 7 Aug. 1860', in Mitchell Library manuscripts, Mss 736 in Microfilm Fm4/3096.

Social Melancholy

For all manner of provocation, it is well worth plunging directly in to the Mitscherlichs' studies. The English translations most readily available are:

Alexander Mitscherlich, *Society without the Father: A Contribution to Social Psychology*, London: Tavistock, 1969.

Alexander and Margarete Mitscherlich, *The Inability to Mourn*, London: Tavistock, 1975.

For readers interested in less 'clinical' accounts of the social and personal pathologies of 'aftermath cultures', consult the following:

Charles S. Maier, *The Unmasterable Past: History, Holocaust, and German National Identity*, Cambridge (Mass): Harvard University Press, 1988.

Eric L. Santner, *Stranded Objects: Mourning, Memory and Film in Postwar Germany*, Ithaca: Cornell University Press, 1990.

Thomas Elsaesser, *New German Cinema: a History*, London: Macmillan, 1989.